ENDORSEMENTS

I read *Christian Family MELTDOWN!* in one day!!!! Spot on with what is happening with the family today! Easy to read and very convicting!! Laid out in simple terms but backed up with scripture for today's too busy lifestyles! Thanks for writing a sequel!

—Dr. Buddy McClung

Christian Family MELTDOWN! is a unique and timely look at the spiritual condition of the American family with a refreshing reminder of God's blueprint for families using relevant scriptures. Readers of Dr. Peters' first book, *Which Way Is Up?* will recognize his pointed wit, hard hitting questions and transparency.

—Helene Marshall

Dr. Mark Peters has done it again. His second book – *Christian Family MELTDOWN!*; delivers another powerful message and is a great continuation of his first book, *Which Way Is Up?* There is no question God is working through Dr. Peters to deliver the Truth about what is ailing our Country today and tearing us apart from God, but he shows how we as Christians can prevail by committing our lives to Jesus Christ and staying in His Word and in prayer every day. Through his writing I have strengthened my relationship with Christ and want to help others who are struggling in their faith.

—Jeff Portwood, Lufkin, TX

Dear Mark, you have touched my heart and conscience once again with your book – *Christian Family MELTDOWN!*

When I was able to pick your manuscript up again, I couldn't put it down.

Through Scriptures, you noted Christ's continued faithfulness and love for me even though I truly am not worthy of it. As well as the fact of His death on the cross for me, a nobody, but special enough that he knows the number of hairs on my head.

It was an eye opener for me that I am not where I should be in my walk with Him either, especially after reading about your mentors mentioned in the book. So many "things" come up and occupy my time when I should be spending more time each day with HIM and studying His Word. The rest is just 'stuff'.

—Janet Jones

I loved the straightforward boldness of *Christian Family MELTDOWN!;* your book about the family; and especially its message concerning heaven and hell. We often see a façade of Christianity that is victim to the tyranny of busyness. Your book beautifully emphasizes that our beliefs strengthen in those things where we spend our time and focus. In relationships, if we focus on the negative . . . we see more negative, if we focus on the positives . . . we see more positives. If we focus on Jesus Christ and His Word . . . we become better servants of our Lord and King! Great message for today's families!

—Scott Logan, D.D.S.

I pray that people stop sacrificing their families, children, marriages and each other on the altar of self-centeredness and start living God centered lives. I pray that our nation turns its face back to God and it starts with Christians not being ashamed of the gospel, not fearing rejection or persecution, and not fearing man but fearing God! It starts with one person at a time. This book – *Christian Family MELTDOWN!*; flies in the face of "easy believeism," which has weakened so many churches, and led to lukewarm Christians who do not want to count the cost. We are all guilty, but through Christ, we can have victory for our families.

—Steve Dwyer

Christian Family MELTDOWN! – brings out God's Word in such a way that if individuals would do what God says, things would work out better for the family unit. It has a timely message for our day given that many families are dysfunctional and would benefit from its message. *Christian Family MELTDOWN!* – holds great insight into what went wrong and what can be done differently as the family faces great challenges today.

—Mary Jo Peters

The book is a reflection of all you have mentored me on over the past twenty years. It took medical issues in my life for God to get my attention because most of the time, for various reasons, I did not want to listen. The change occurred once I began the discipline of reading the Bible EVERY morning and praying. Then I wanted to be back in church . . . then I wanted to be involved in ministry.

Slowly I am being transformed into the family spiritual leader I should have been. God has helped me to reduce my self-centerdness. I felt the book tracks many of the thought processes as the Holy Spirit transforms your life. No doubt it is a life long process, but there is peace in knowing you are on the right track and you are seeing life be better.

—Joseph McCollum

If you are hungry for a politically correct, philosophy du jour on manhood, the family, and faith you will find this book hard to swallow. But, if you want to hear what the Creator of the universe has to say about manhood, if you are starving for a life of purpose and fulfillment, Mark's words will be music to your ears and bread for your soul.

—Dr. Jay Gross, West Conroe Baptist Church

Christian Family
MELTDOWN!
Are All Men Idiots?

Mark Peters

LUCIDBOOKS

First Printing: 2014

ISBN-10: 1632960079
ISBN-13: 978-1-63296-007-8

Special Sales: Most Lucid Books titles are available in special quantity discounts. Custom imprinting or excerpting can also be done to fit special needs. Contact Lucid Books at info@lucidbooks.net.

DEDICATION

I dedicate this book to my loving wife, Keyea. The one person in my life, besides Jesus Christ, who knows the absolute knucklehead sinner that I am . . . and loves me in spite of it! Your "staying the course" with me has made me better than I ever could have been without you and your influence on my life! I love you, Sweetie!

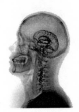

TABLE OF CONTENTS

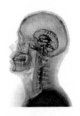

PREFACE

Some of you who read *Which Way is Up?* are probably saying to yourself, "Here we go again, where is Mark going with this book?"

Alright, let me explain. On our way home from dinner with the kids one night, I was stopped at a traffic light waiting for it to turn green. I looked at the bumper sticker on the car in front of us and just busted out laughing. Keyea, my wife asked, "What's so funny?"

I said, "Look at that bumper sticker on the car in front of us." She took a look, broke out into a laugh and said, "I want one of those! Where can I get one?"

I'll let you in on the joke. The bumper sticker said: "All Men Are Idiots – And I Married Their King!"

That bumper sticker slogan stuck with me and I couldn't shake it from my mind. Every time I thought about it, I just cracked up laughing. It rolled over and over in my mind. What was the underlying meaning? I wondered: the lady driving the car sporting that sticker, what was her marriage like? How did her husband feel about his wife blaring this message about him in such a sarcastic and derogatory way for all those driving behind her to see? I wondered what their kids thought of the bumper sticker message. Was this family like so many families we see around us each day – broken?

Then I thought about my own marriage and family. Was Keyea serious? Would she really like that bumper sticker on the back of her car? And why did she laugh so hard when she saw it? Maybe there was a message for me there on that bumper . . .

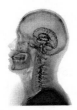

INTRODUCTION

So are all men idiots? Well, that seems to be how men are portrayed on the commercials, sitcoms, and in the media in general. The more I thought about it– there was a message on that bumper sticker – and a prevalent one.

What is the message? And what are we as families doing to promote or suppress the message that belittles the supposed head of the family? Certainly women make mistakes and poor decisions too, don't they? These were questions worth thinking about.

That's when I decided to go ahead and make that bumper sticker slogan the title of one of the Sunday-School lessons I was going to teach. The lesson was one of a four part series I had put together on marriage and the family. It has been well received and presented numerous times, in differing scopes, and at different venues. The crux of the message is that there is an attack on the family in our country and we lack a relationship with our Lord and Savior in this busy nation of ours. This lack of relationship with Christ weakens our relationship with our spouse, as well as the rest of the family. Christian families desire to succeed in carrying on the love of our Savior and country, and to take some steps to retrieve our families from the decimation around us.

We all know that our nation has a catastrophic problem. A problem so prevalent, that we see the evidence of the destruction and breakdown of our country before our very eyes. That problem is that Satan is waging a battle on the family in our country and around the world. The decline of the family unit is plaguing our nation and bringing it to its knees in many ways: divorce, kids having kids, blended families, children born out of wedlock, and mother's & father's not taking responsibility for their own children. Often what accompanies the breakdown of the family is financial hardships, broken promises, and broken kids who have no stable set of parents to look up to, and be trained by. When the marriages do stay together, it seems they are more of a partnership, cohabitation, or necessity of convenience rather than a loving and vibrant relationship with a father who steps into the role of being the spiritual leader of his family with Jesus Christ at its center. The monthly bills and finances take precedence over everything else, making for stressful relationships and the likelihood the marriage will end up on the rocks anyway. Our society, culture, and environment have, in many ways, enabled and pressed men into the dubious role of abdicating their responsibility of being the spiritual leaders of their families.

That's what this book is about. The family that Baby Boomers remember is going the way of the record album, the eight-track tape, and the cassette. In a similar way, the family is becoming obsolete and unrecognizable, and the future doesn't look very promising either. What can we do to turn this gigantic problem around? Let's see what God and His Word have to say about all this and see if, with His instruction, we can find some answers together to these pressing questions.

But first, I should add another disclaimer. If anyone should carry the moniker "idiot" – it would be me . . . Why do you think my wife was so ready to try to find one of those bumper stickers? Like all families, mine is not perfect and has some dysfunction in its midst . . . just as ALL families do. If you don't think there is dysfunction in your family, go to the last chapter of my first book that describes how we, as broken and sinful human beings "lie to ourselves."

As well, please know that I have three prayers for you who are reading this book and I pray these pretty much every day:

- That you would be drawn into a relationship with Jesus Christ as your Lord and Savior / or to a closer relationship with Him – because that is the most important decision for all of us.

- That you would be drawn into His Holy Word . . . the Bible – because so many Christians don't spend any time in it.

- That through these first two and prayer – you would be filled with the Holy Spirit and enabled more readily to share the gospel of Jesus Christ with those that He sends across your path.

Okay, now we're ready to go forward . . . let's go see where this bumper sticker slogan takes us on revealing the "MELTDOWN!" of the Christian family.

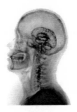

CHAPTER 1 – ALL

A re "ALL" men idiots? Where it started is anyone's guess – mine included. Where did it get into people's minds that men are just "knots on a log" with virtually no redeeming qualities to speak of? Was it in the 60's, when the "peace, love, dove" movement started? Was it when women's liberation was coming to the forefront of our culture? How about going back to the time when women were struggling to even have the right to vote? After all, women weren't just servants and maids, brought into the marriage to raise the kids, take care of the house, place slippers on their husband's feet, and serve him a cocktail – or were they? There's really no telling when it actually started. Why, it could have even been at the very start, say when Adam and Eve were in the garden. Who took the first bite of the fruit, and who followed the leader? We could make a case for Adam being the first husband to not exercise his leadership role right there in the garden. I wonder if Eve would say the fall was all Adam's fault. Let's see what the Scriptures say.

Genesis 1:26-27 – Then God said, "Let Us make man in Our image, according to Our likeness; and let them rule over the fish of the sea and over the birds of the

sky and over the cattle and over all the earth, and over every creeping thing that creeps on the earth." [27] And God created man in His own image, in the image of God He created him; male and female He created them.

So we know God created us in His image and according to His likeness, and gave man authority over the creatures on the earth. The thing that is obvious here is that God has a plan. God has had a plan from the get-go – even from before the get was to go. God's plan had an order to it and nothing could change His plan, just as nothing can change that plan for eternity. Our question is: How do we each fit into His plan? That is the question most of us fail to acknowledge or think about in our hectic and fast-paced frenzy of a life. In our self-centered / self-serving culture, we don't even have a clue that our Lord and Savior has a purpose for our lives – EACH ONE of OUR LIVES!

We each have a purpose and we each have a role to play – or not. What is that role? There is an order and there is the right way for God's plan to be carried out in our civilization. It involves the FAMILY. But wait a minute, even if there is a plan laid out by God, it sure doesn't mean we each have to follow that plan. After all, He does give us the freedom to choose Him and His plan, as well as the freedom to decide that we want no part of Him. God does love us too much to force Himself on us, and He has no need for relationship with "automatons" who answer to His beckoning. No, He desires those who choose Him over themselves and their own wills to live to themselves. This makes the way for the disparity and struggle that we each find our families in while on this big blue marble we call earth.

Satan has waged a war on the family that is seemingly taking our world and turning it upside down in a lot of people's minds. His war on the family unit is relentless and wreaking havoc in untold myriads of people groups around the world. His onslaught is rampant, it's formidable, and it is devastating among us. Yes, Satan is a masterful and worthy opponent to the holiness and good that God intends, but he has to be there – or there wouldn't be a choice to make. Fortunately for us, he is ultimately defeated.

Let me ask you something dear reader. Have you or your friends come from broken and dysfunctional families? Many, if not all have been decimated by misguided quests for the happiness the world portrays. This pursuit of a false happiness has only led to heartbreak and the resultant dissolution of what could have been a wonderful family devoted to God, one another, and the service of other strong families around us. Instead, we end up with alimony and child-support, custody hearings, arguments over who gets who when, and children caught in the middle of some bizarre, complex, selfish dance.

The happiness that the world sells is a farce and a lie, peddled by the father of lies, Satan himself. Jesus Christ, and no one else, should be the center of our families! Now hold on a minute, before you think about throwing out this book because I'm getting "too personal," hear me out, it will make sense. Give me a chance to speak 'heart to heart' with you about this GINORMOUS elephant that is in the room of our society. The family is not just broken, but is facing extinction!

Do you think this was God's intention when he decided to give Adam a wife? Let's see what the Bible has to say about this.

Genesis 2:18 – Then the LORD God said, "It is not good for the man to be alone; I will make him a helper suitable for him."

Now just think about this. Could God have just said, "You know, Adam – I've been thinking . . . and I think it's not so good for you to be by yourself on this earth I've created for you. I think I'll go ahead and make a suitable partner for you, so I'm going to go over here and get another little pile of dust and form that suitable partner." Number one, God has never been surprised or been found lacking for anything, and He never will be. Number two, God made all of creation, just the way He intended to – with His perfect plan in mind.

Part of that perfect plan included putting Adam into a deep sleep, and taking a "part" of him, his rib, and using it to fashion man's helpmate. This then provides us the example that God meant us to have – that woman comes from man as a rib, is "custom-built" by God as the absolute perfect "fit" for man, which leads to them having the God-given ability to come together to become "one flesh" again and procreate, and their offspring will do the same.

Human beings have messed it up and not done a very good job of carrying out God's plan though. We had our own ideas about what we should do with our differences – as well as with our likenesses. Just read **Romans chapter 1** for some insight into this. God gave us a freewill to choose Him, or not to do so.

That's the thing about freewill and not being created as "robots," with no discernment, discretion, or ability to choose who we serve. God made us in His image of which gives us a body, soul, and spirit. We have a conscience, and an ability to make decisions, both right and wrong ones. We know that we have the ability to choose, but what is driving the choices we make? Adam and Eve made a choice, and they both made the wrong one – to ignore and do what God had given them specific directions not to do. And that is, they ate of that tree.

It's much like what we do today. We want it "our way" or no way – and definitely not God's way!

Let me ask you another question: when was the last time you made a decision that you knew was in direct disobedience to what God wants? The truth is, we're failing in this all the time. It could be that a thought has raced across your mind that you know is a sin, even in the last instant. Part of our problem, as pointed out in my first book, is that we are all very good and adept at lying to ourselves. We don't want to take an honest and in-depth look at who we are and acknowledge what truly depraved sinners we are, and how absolutely sovereign God is. Hence we call ourselves "wise" without knowing what true wisdom is.

James 1:5 – But if any of you lacks wisdom, let him ask of God, who gives to all men generously and without reproach, and it will be given to him.

True wisdom comes only from God and His Holy Word. Many would argue this point and laugh it off that someone would make such a statement. According to most dictionaries, wisdom is a combination of KNOWLEDGE, INSIGHT, and JUDGMENT. Knowledge is the accumulated philosophic or scientific learning type. Insight is the ability to discern inner qualities and relationships. Judgment is how to use these with good sense. As important as knowledge, insight, and judgment each is, none of it is worth anything without the all-important addendum "in Christ." Many will scoff at this notion – "What do you mean 'in Christ?'" or "Where do you come off saying wisdom comes only from God and the Bible?"

Take fifteen or twenty minutes to read **1 Corinthians chapter 1** and the first five **Proverbs**, and you'll get an inkling as to why true wisdom is only found "in Christ". No one attains true wisdom without the Holy Spirit revealing it to them through God's Holy Word and prayer – no one.

Yes, people can attain much knowledge and intelligence on varieties of different topics, but true wisdom is only of God – and His perfect will and plan. Our job is not to determine God's perfect will and plan, but to bring our lives under Him and His Son Jesus Christ, through the indwelling Holy Spirit – to be used as a servant to help His plan come about – for His glory. God gives us the opportunity to do this, but He also gives the option to refuse Him and His plan, which many of us do. In this struggle to find wisdom – either in Christ or in the world – the family is impacted in a variety of ways.

God has a plan for the family. And He reveals it in numerous places in His Scriptures. One of the first mentions comes in the early part of Genesis.

Genesis 2:24 – For this cause a man shall leave his father and his mother, and shall cleave to his wife; and they shall become one flesh.

They are a dying phenomenon and becoming more nonexistent by the minute. The chances are you may know of some of them, but actually don't have anyone in your family who even remembers their example. They are the kindred spirits, the love-birds, the couple who have been married for 50 years or more. It's so sweet to see them – still in love, still with that twinkle in their eyes for one another, still holding hands as they walk or sit with one another. Shoot, they're even starting to look like one another when they've been together for that long! (My wife is very sad about this being a possibility for she and I, but I'm all for it!)

You see, these couples have "gotten it" – they "know the program" – and "stuck with it for the duration!" They know that marriage is "hard work" and they also discover something else, something most people involved in marriage never discover because they have never been married long enough to find out. They truly do become "one flesh" with one another.

"One flesh" is an interesting concept. It doesn't seem to fit with the dual career, and upwardly mobile track that we find on most couple's minds these days. In our striving for bigger homes, nicer cars, more income, and more activities for our kids, seeking out to become "one flesh" has taken the back seat. Instead of focusing on our marriages, our focus has been on everything but, and when this happens, tyranny runs amok within the family. Tyranny of the urgent, tyranny of possessions, tyranny of the self! All of these, plus many others rob our attention from where it should rightfully be.

> **Romans 3:10-18 – As it is written, "There is none righteous, not even one; [11] There is none who understands, There is none who seeks for God; [12] All have turned aside, together they have become useless; There is none who does good, There is not even one." [13] "Their throat is an open grave, With their tongues they keep deceiving," "The poison of asps is under their lips"; [14] "Whose mouth is full of cursing and bitterness"; [15] "Their feet are swift to shed blood, [16] Destruction and misery are in their paths, [17] And the path of peace have they not known." [18] "There is no fear of God before their eyes."**

With their tongues they keep deceiving . . .

I'm a dentist, so I get lots of conversation time with patients. Many of them have told me stories about their kids "shacking-up" with other kids! (I call them kids, but they may be sixteen to thirty years old.) Some of the most familiar comments sound a little like this: "Oh, they're getting married in about a year or so . . ."

Yeah, right! Tell me how those marriages are doing five years from now. Chances are they have moved on to another partner and they're "gonna get married" to them as well. They've quite possibly added a kid or two into the mix also. Our families are being ruined, destroyed, and broken down in so many ways and on so many fronts that we can't even keep up. The days of Ward and June Cleaver – of *Leave it to Beaver* fame have gone far, far away in our society and culture. The days of Mom staying at home being the housewife and Dad bringing home the bacon to the loving family with the daughter helping her Mom bake the cookies while the son tends his paper route is caput!

Well get ready, because one day we are all going to get the wake-up call of our lives! Yes husbands and wives, it matters not your gender, we will all have to give an account before our Lord and Savior.

Matthew 16:27 – "For the Son of Man is going to come in the glory of His Father with His angels; and will then recompense every man according to his deeds."

Are you ready for this guaranteed and certain event? You can scoff all you want, but mark His Word (my words don't count like His), you will give an account of your actions and behavior to the one true God of the universe. Our accountability will be clear to us, and our judgment will be sure if we haven't received Jesus Christ as our Lord and Savior. It will be evident that God knows us even better than we know ourselves and we will stand in awe that we could have been so prideful and arrogant that we felt the God of the universe could have been fooled. Do you know what will really surprise us at this moment of true judgment from our God? It will be that we have so belittled the love He has had for us all along. That love, which we chose to ignore and reject all through our lives will be so apparent and pervasive, that we will be driven to our faces in front of Him begging His forgiveness and mercy to us depraved and self-centered sinners.

> **Hebrews 4:13 – And there is no creature hidden from His sight, but all things are open and laid bare to the eyes of Him with whom we have to do.**

> **Romans 14:11-12 – For it is written, "As I live, says the Lord, every knee shall bow to Me, And every tongue shall give praise to God." ¹² So then each one of us shall give account of himself to God."**

There will be no hiding places to run to and no rocks to crawl under. Escape from His judgment on sin will be unavoidable, sure and just. God sees all, and knows all – He is omniscient. Our lives are an open book for God to look over and review as to what we have done and not done for Him. Not only are we responsible for the things we have done – and the ways we have sinned – but we are also responsible for those He has sent our way while we lived our short-winded lives. When judgment comes, we'll be aghast at how flippant we were throughout our lives – not only to His desires and wants for us, but how we treated those He sent our way as well. These were lost opportunities for the furthering of His kingdom and perfect plan for our lives. Opportunities squandered while seeking to further ourselves and our own selfish ambitions.

Mark 8:38 – "For whoever is ashamed of Me and My words in this adulterous and sinful generation, the Son of Man will also be ashamed of him when He comes in the glory of His Father with the holy angels."

How will we feel when we see all the times that we were ashamed to even acknowledge Jesus Christ as Who He really is – God of the universe! Won't it be sad; won't it be tragic when He is ashamed of us? We had the chances placed right in front of our collective and individual noses. Chances to share Him and His gospel with those we came in contact with each and every day. Instead, we make excuses and say things like, "you know how hard it is to broach the subject of something as important as one's religion or faith." Or "I just couldn't bring myself to do it," we might say.

Well, guess who's ashamed now?

Our lives are about relationships: those with our God and Savior, as well as those with the people around us. We seem to be struggling at maintaining both of these relationships don't we?

John 6:37 – "All that the Father gives Me shall come to Me, and the one who comes to Me I will certainly not cast out.

Jesus knows His own and they know Him. The believers in Christ can rest assured that they are one with the Father, Son, and Holy Spirit for eternity. They will never be cast out from God's presence. Look in **John chapter 10** to see how no one and nothing can snatch us believers out of Jesus Christ's, or His Father's hand.

But still there are some who ask the question, "How could a loving God send anyone to hell for eternity?"

Let me ask you a question: If God saved no one, would He be justified? I'll ask it again a little differently: If the God of the universe saved no one from their sin, would He be justified? I had never really contemplated this question before, until a Pastor challenged me with it. This question begs an answer from all of us and most of the people that I know whom I would consider to be strong in their faith in Christ would answer the question with an unequivocal "YES." Yes, God would be justified if He saved no one from their sin. If this is the case, then we could go on to ask the next question, "Why then, is it wrong for a loving God to choose to save those who would willingly come to faith in Him under His grace and accept His offer of salvation through His Son Jesus Christ?"

One thing we should be able to set as a precedent that is startling to some who haven't taken a close look at themselves in light of the holiness of the God of the universe. That is the fact that "ALL" men (and women by the way), are sinners and are under the judgment of God's righteous wrath. That is unless they are sinless and uphold every iota of God's law – perfectly. We will "ALL" be held accountable for our sins at judgment day. Either you live a life perfectly good and sinless on your own; or you will need a substitutionary and perfect sacrifice to pay the price for you to the Holy God for all your sins. In the end, we "ALL" make a choice. Either we are good enough on our own, or we accept the grace offered by our loving God through His Son's shed blood on the Cross for our sins.

CHOOSE WISELY!

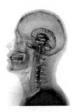

CHAPTER 2 – MEN

I know this book is seemingly addressed mainly to the men, but don't think you are off the hook ladies. Actually, you have your part in this debacle as well. There is more than enough blame to be handed and passed around to both the men and the women. If we are honest with ourselves, we will not overlook the fact that each of us has dropped the ball in regard to our own contributions to losing the family unit. It started long, long ago . . . back at the beginning in fact . . .

> **Genesis 3:1-6 – Now the serpent was more crafty than any beast of the field which the LORD God had made. And he said to the woman, "Indeed, has God said, 'You shall not eat from any tree of the garden '?" ² And the woman said to the serpent, "From the fruit of the trees of the garden we may eat; ³ but from the fruit of the tree which is in the middle of the garden, God has said, 'You shall not eat from it or touch it, lest you die.'" ⁴ And the serpent said to the woman, "You surely shall not die! ⁵ "For God knows that in the day you eat from it your eyes will be opened, and you will be like God, knowing good and evil." ⁶ When the woman saw that the tree was good for food, and that it was a**

delight to the eyes, and that the tree was desirable to make *one* wise, she took from its fruit and ate; and she gave also to her husband with her, and he ate.

This was the start of our first disobedience to God Himself. Many call this occurrence "The Fall." This one act of defiance by these two who had become one flesh, led to the two of them being separated from God and kicked out of the Garden of Eden. It also contributed to discord amongst the two of them, and to their descendants being born with their acquired sin nature. Wow! Talk about getting more than you bargained for! Adam and Eve thought they were just going to be having their eyes opened & made wiser, and that seemed like a good thing. They didn't realize all the ramifications of this catastrophic decision. We do the same thing don't we?

I hear patients and friends all the time who share with me their circumstances and the decisions they are confronted with. Often, the decision is one in which the best answer is plainly laid out in God's Holy Word. But the problem for most people is that they have spent no time in the Bible. Thus they are leading themselves off God's will and path – the path He intended for their lives. Others read the Bible, but only the parts they agree with. They pick and choose their verses out of the Bible, and don't believe it is all the true Word of God, and they run aground somewhere down their path as well.

I had a friend tell me that the most popular song sung at funerals is – "I Did It My Way" by Frank Sinatra. Our culture prides itself in choosing our own destinies. Satan, as well as our sin nature, has us so saturated in self-love that we don't really recognize when we are prideful. You know, Satan doesn't mark the roads he sets before us with a sign that reads, "This is the way to hell!" He's too sly and deceptive to do that.

So we set out on our own, and way too many times are on the wrong path.

With our eyes seeing but not really seeing, we make decisions with wrong motives and desires. The problem is that we give no consideration to our Lord and Savior Jesus Christ, and His will for our decisions in life. And I'm talking about both men and women.

I mentioned in my first book how I've ordered Bibles for friends and acquaintances through the years. I have their name imprinted on them, put tabs in them to locate the different books easily, and underline or star the Scripture References located on the page at the end of this book. Let me share with you several stories of how these episodes have turned out so far.

"Life's too good . . ."

Years ago I was out and about with a friend that I'd given one of these Bibles to a few months earlier. I asked him if he'd cracked that Bible open and taken a look at it. His response was intriguing. He said, "No Mark, life is too good and I haven't really needed to do so." Wow, and I thought I was cocky!

It's sad when we get diverted with the blessings in our lives. Couple that with our sinful state and we often don't even feel our own depravity and need for a Savior. We say, "Life is too good, man! I'm having too much fun!" All the while we are blinded to the sin in our lives and our sinful influence on others. Food for thought, wouldn't you say?

This same gentleman, the one I gave the Bible to, was in my office sobbing about ten years later, when his child was diagnosed with a life-long, debilitating disease. No, I'm sure the Bible still sits in its unopened state, but the comfort it could provide is not taken in, and the relief it could instill is brushed-back and discarded. Oh, he's dealing with his son's disease okay, I suppose. He just doesn't have the perspective that the Lord would provide him with if he would avail himself to Him.

"Still in the box . . ."

There are other instances in which I have given Bibles to friends. I used to leave the new Bibles in the original box. I quit doing that. One time while I was visiting a friend, I was perusing his study looking at the books on the bookshelves. I looked down and noticed a box for a study Bible that looked like the one I'd given him. It was on the bottom shelf next to the floor. I thought, "Surely not . . ." There it was, the Bible I had given him years earlier was still untouched and in the box. My heart sank as I looked at God's Holy Word, the gentleman's name was embossed on the cover, tabs had been placed and taped on both sides, Scriptures had been underlined with a ballpoint pen, and a nice little note written on the inside of the front cover. The note was a request to not let the Bible sit on a shelf and collect dust. Oh well, I guess the box was keeping the dust off of it anyway. I wondered if he ever even read my note.

"Best gift I ever received . . ."

But not everyone has treated a gifted Bible in the same way. At the other end of the spectrum, let me tell you about Alfred. Alfred is an immigrant to this country and proud to have just received his green card, which took some doing. Not being able to practice medicine as he and his wife did in his home country, they had to resort to waiting tables at restaurants in order to support themselves and their two kids. Coincidently, our church had done outreach at the school that Alfred's children attended. He was touched by the church's generosity, so Alfred and family came to visit our church. When they heard the gospel message preached, they were totally convicted as a family and all came down the aisle and received Jesus Christ as their Lord and Savior.

One night, my wife Keyea and I were having dinner at the restaurant where Alfred worked. He was helping us at our table, and brought by his Bible and opened it up to show it to me. He said, "Dr. Mark I have such a difficult time reading this small print in this Bible. I go home at 10:00 each night and spend three hours until 1:00 reading from it. It gives me a headache from trying to focus on the small print. My wife and I both are finding this to be the case." I replied, "Alfred, I've got you covered . . . write down the correct spelling for you and your wife's names for me." I bought them each large print Bibles, got them all prepared for them and took them to the restaurant to drop them off.

At church, and repeatedly at the restaurant, Alfred and his wife have both come up and told me, "Dr. Mark, you give me the best gift I ever received in my life!" What a thought, the gift of a Bible – the Living Word. It is the best gift a person can receive other than their salvation through Jesus Christ. That is, if that person will read that Bible. Then the Lord can train them up and use them to further His kingdom, but for those leaving it sitting on the shelf . . . not so much.

I haven't kept count of the Bibles I've put together for people this way, but let me tell you about one other time I gave one out; and the results of it . . .

Tommy is a young patient, about twelve or thirteen years old. He came into the office to get his teeth cleaned, and had to come back for a visit to get some fillings. At first, he was pretty quiet, but we were able to visit with one another a little bit and I offered him a copy of *Which Way Is Up?* He took it and his Mother said he began reading it as soon as he got it. When he finished the book he decided to do a book report on it for his school assignment. His Mother said he got the highest grade in the class, and that the report was such that his teacher asked Tommy to loan him the book to read afterward. When his Mom told me that story, I offered to put a Bible together for him, and did so. When I gave it to him he held it as if he was given a treasure! He ran his finger over his name embossed on the front cover. We didn't have much time to visit the day his Mother brought him by to get it, as I had other patients to see when he came by, so he thanked me and left.

Later, his Mother emailed me to tell me that Tommy reads from that Bible every day and even takes it with him to school each day as well. The next time he came into the office guess what he was carrying? He had that Bible under his arm and the cover was scratched up, the tabs were almost mutilated, and the edges of the pages were worn and the corners frayed. He'd been taking that Bible to school every day and reading from it, as well as sharing his faith with his classmates. He showed me how much he had progressed in reading it front to back and I was impressed.

Tommy has told me that it's as if his eyes have been opened . . . and they have. He has availed himself to his Lord and Savior and seeks His presence in relationship, prayer, and His Word each day. Eyes opened. Imagine that!

> Isaiah 35:4-6 – Say to those with anxious heart, "Take courage, fear not. Behold, your God will come *with* vengeance; The recompense of God will come, But He will save you." [5] Then the eyes of the blind will be opened, And the ears of the deaf will be unstopped. [6] Then the lame will leap like a deer, And the tongue of the dumb will shout for joy. For waters will break forth in the wilderness And streams in the Arabah.

It is true that a lot of people in this world don't want their eyes opened. They don't want them to be opened because they know they will not like what they see. Part of the reason people don't want to open their eyes or spend time in their search for the real truth of Jesus Christ and His gospel . . . is that the truth of His Word will cause them to have to look at their own lives, along with their own families.

Genesis 3:7-8 – Then the eyes of both of them were opened, and they knew that they were naked; and they sewed fig leaves together and made themselves loin coverings. ⁸ They heard the sound of the Lord God walking in the garden in the cool of the day, and the man and his wife hid themselves from the presence of the Lord God among the trees of the garden.

We don't like looking at our lives because it makes us look introspectively at ourselves and then ponder what we believe in. If we start to spend time reading and studying the Bible, our eyes are opened much like Adam and Eve's were. Our eyes are opened to the reality of our own depravity and sin, for which, we know that we have need of a Savior. And guess what? We don't like to depend on anyone else, or to have to be ashamed of our nakedness before God. Instead, we prefer to hide our sins and keep them hidden from the omnipotent God of the universe . . . Who by the way, knows all of our sins anyway.

Genesis 3:9-12 – Then the Lord God called to the man, and said to him, "Where are you?" ¹⁰ He said, "I heard the sound of You in the garden, and I was afraid because I was naked; so I hid myself." ¹¹ And He said, "Who told you that you were naked? Have you eaten from the tree of which I commanded you not to eat?" ¹² The man said, "The woman whom You

gave *to be* with me, she gave me from the tree, and I ate."

Now we get to the fun . . . or not so fun part. It's the ol' – "He said . . . she said" gamesmanship that our sin nature is so prone to. The Fall sets up quite well how the trappings of our society deals with personal responsibility. In our society, it's as if everyone is the "victim" and no one is accountable for what they've done. Instead, like Adam and Eve, we cover ourselves and our actions in the best possible light, and we cover the darkness of our sin within and without . . . or so we think.

Men, we can play all the blame games we want. We can claim that the women's lib movement absolves us from all responsibility for being the spiritual leaders of our family. We can claim that the cards are stacked against us or that we are to be the primary "bread winners" for our family so we don't have time . . . you pick it. But each of these excuses will not remove our responsibility. Inevitably, we men are accountable before God for the sin of not taking up the mantel of leading our family for Christ. Remember, we will "all" have to give an account.

Genesis 3:13 – Then the LORD God said to the woman, "What is this you have done?" And the woman said, "The serpent deceived me, and I ate."

Some of you ladies have been deceived into believing that you need to "wear the pants" in the family: that you need to have the career, be the head of the family, and prove yourself to the world. The world would have you prove that you are indeed not going to be put into the position to submit to anyone. If you've fallen for that lie, it may mean you're also not being submissive to our Lord and His Word as well. Satan is a pretty clever dude isn't he? What better way to sabotage the marriage and the family than to pit the husband and the wife against one another. If he could pull that off and get the two of them arguing over who's in charge, it's a done deal. Then the case is closed and you can wrap it up and tie it with a bow.

Guess what? He's done it, and it's paying off in spades! No one can agree on who's in charge, and while the dispute rages on, the spiritual leadership of the family is left to no one. The husband throws up his hands and says, "You want the kids to go to church? Get after it . . . I'm goin' fishin', or huntin', or to the golf course. After all, I work all week and need some down time. You train 'em up in all that 'holy moly' stuff!"

The husband may be so out of tune with whatever he believes, that he starts to ridicule his wife for even making the effort to get them all to church. The wife, determined to do her best to get her kids involved in a walk of faith and in the presence of their Lord and Savior, persists as best she can. But it's such a hard task that she may fall through the cracks in getting them there herself, and no one ends up going to church . . . it just doesn't seem worth the effort.

If, on the other hand, there was a common commitment of both the spouse's walk of faith, then there would be a team with common goals of growing not only the kids, but themselves as well, in their relationship with Christ. Then the parents might be able to follow the template set out in these verses . . .

Ephesians 5:21-25 – and be subject to one another in the fear of Christ. [22] Wives, *be subject* to your own husbands, as to the Lord. [23] For the husband is the head of the wife, as Christ also is the head of the church,

He Himself *being* **the Savior of the body.** [24] **But as the church is subject to Christ, so also the wives** *ought to be* **to their husbands in everything.** [25] **Husbands, love your wives, just as Christ also loved the church and gave Himself up for her,**

Ladies have you ever even thought about asking your husband to be the spiritual leader of your family? Do you even want him to do so? Have you asked him to take on this imperative and vital responsibility? If so, have you followed through on enabling him to act on it, by helping him do this job? Chances are by observation, that the majority of the wives out there have not ever considered or asked these vitally important questions. The media has portrayed us men as dunces and idiots so long, maybe we are actually buying into it ourselves. Thus we don't even think of taking up the mantel for our families.

Why wouldn't we come up with the idea that it is important for us to train up our kids in their faith in Christ? One reason we men don't is that most of us have not had that attitude and example modeled to us in our own childhood from our Dad. Most of us men didn't have a father who was trained up to be the spiritual leader of his family by his own father. The result is that the bad habits of generations keep getting passed down and down, further and further, more and more ingrained into the fabric of our poorly led families. This then perpetuates the same dysfunctional tendencies right on down the line from fathers to sons, as well as mothers to daughters, and the cycle continues. This cycle needs to be broken, but the strong chain link we have to break to get out of that cycle always seems to be getting more and more unbreakable.

The result is poor leadership and examples of poor faith and poor family tendencies, which propagate more of the same dysfunction down the line in our families. Like it or not, we are training up our kids to be just like us, and most of the time that likeness is not very desirable. It's not that we want our kids to be just like us. Most of us parents truly don't want our kids to do as we do – we want them to do as we say, because we know we are not living the life we should be living either. When we do this, we're continually lying to ourselves . . . and our kids.

To further illustrate this point, I have found that it goes not only from parents to their kids, but the other way as well. Let me share with you what I've been having happen to me over and over during the last several years. This is a widespread occurrence that I've been inundated with time and again from young men, as well as older ones and the ladies too. The situation they come to me with goes like this, "Mark, my Dad has never been real keen on going to church and it seems his Dad was not strong in his faith either, so I'm in a bit of a quandary. Since I've received Jesus Christ as my Lord and Savior, I want to share my faith with him in order to help him go to heaven as well. Can you tell me how I can share my faith with my Dad? I'm really struggling with how to visit with him about Jesus Christ."

I can relate, because I had to do the same thing with my Dad. My Dad didn't have an example of a strong spiritual leader of a father in his life because his Dad left and was gone from their family when he was six years old. Dad did the best he could without having the example of a father strong in Christ. He would always say a prayer before our meals, but he didn't speak of his faith at all that I can remember growing up. Oh we went to church sporadically, but weren't regular attenders.

Later in life when Keyea and I had moved to Conroe, he was staying with us while he was going through some treatments for some medical problems he'd been having. One day as I was driving him home I got up the courage (through prayer) to say to him, "Dad . . . I've got to ask you the toughest question I've ever had to ask you in my life. If you died today – where would you be tomorrow?"

He said, "Well I'm not sure, Mark."

I replied, "Then we need to talk, Dad . . . because I know where I would be – and that would be in heaven with Jesus Christ and the saints for eternity. I love you Dad and want to make sure that you are there as well. After all, we are all going to spend eternity in one of two places . . . and I want you in heaven with me." This at least opened the door for the subsequent discussions that Dad & I were able to have about our faith. He died about 7 years later and I look forward to seeing him again someday!

Many people have a hard time discussing their faith with other people anyway, and seemingly more so with their own family members. One thing I can relate to you is that once you break the ice and share your faith with a few of those around you, you will be amazed at how often you start seeing the opportunities come your way. Also, the sharing will come easier and easier for you.

But most of us don't pursue our own faith, much less train up our kids – or share it with friends and family members. Often times we are so very busy that we just can't seem to make the time to spend in relationship with our Savior each day. This dilemma seems to be from the "collection of the tyrannies." The tyranny of the "urgent" – the veritable menagerie of pressing tasks and busy-ness agendas that we work ourselves into. The tyranny of "possessions" – how much of our time is occupied obtaining and taking care of stuff we acquire, but don't really need? We sometimes do this for the sake of having something to do in order to feel we are being productive with our time. The tyranny of "meaningless conversation" – do we truly need to go about sowing discord to those around us . . . by telling them that our neighbor is not meeting up to our standard of what the perfect neighbor should be like . . . because their lawn is not up to our standards? The tyranny of "self-centeredness" – such as, "I know that I've told you quite a bit about myself, so now, let's hear what great things you have to say about me?" The tyranny of "what will others think" – they will think I'm weak if I don't do such and such. If I share my faith in Christ with them, they might not want to be my friend anymore . . .

Our minds are so cluttered with the meaningless, the mundane, and ourselves that we never really come up for air and ask the really important questions. Like, why am I here? Where will I spend eternity? Where will my family and friends spend eternity? How can I grow closer to my Lord and Savior and be transformed more and more into His likeness? What purpose does He have for my life this side of heaven? How can my spouse and I grow in our individual walks of faith thus enabling us to grow in Christ as a couple? Are my spouse and I truly "walking the walk" of our faith in Christ . . . or are we just "talking the talk" and going through the motions of being Christians? Who will Jesus bring across my path today to share Him and His gospel with? Will I be looking for opportunities to share Christ with those I meet today? Will I seize those opportunities and be bold for the One Who paid the price for my own redemption and reconciliation to He, and the Father? How can I be a "servant" – as Jesus was, of those I come in contact with today? Will I look for chances to listen to them, really hear their concerns, and actually pray for them?

Yes, we are all deceived and drawn away from our Lord and Savior, away from His will for our lives, and away from the priorities that He set for our families. Consequently, the family unit is broken, splintered, and barely limps along under the guise of – "Oh yeah, we're doing great . . . everything's great . . . really great! No problems with our family . . . we're great!" All the while we aren't great, and we live out our lives of quiet desperation just hoping others don't find out how really broken our marriages are, as are our kids, and our own lives. We are "living the lie" espoused in my first book, putting on the façade of, "We are GREAT! . . . and just why isn't your family as great as ours?"

The Fall brought about even more problems for us men and women to consider . . .

Genesis 3:16 – To the woman He said, "I will greatly multiply Your pain in childbirth, In pain you shall bring forth children; Yet your desire shall be for your husband, And he shall rule over you."

While some women have broken free of the desire of a husband, most have not as of yet? Or have they? It seems the desire to get married and be tied to someone for the rest of their lives has decreased in popularity over the last few decades hasn't it? They might say, "Why not just live together and see if I really want to give myself to this guy for the rest of my life? If it doesn't work out . . . then 'no harm-no foul' and I'll move on to the next one. Who knows, one of these days I may find the right one."

Or they may say, "Are you serious??? You want ME to get married and let this guy RULE OVER ME? I don't think so! I've got my own ideas about what I want to do with my life. Don't expect me to give up my rights as the one who determines the type of life and family I want to have. I can handle it on my own if I have to . . . without the input of this loser I'd be tied to."

Not getting married is an option if we want to cohabitate and live in continual sin before the world and our Savior. God's design and plan was for the marriage covenant between a man and a woman in order that they would propagate and populate the earth . . . and stay together for life. The family unit is the building block for everything in our society. Sure there are those called to live a celibate and single life. But we sure seem to have broken-up the marriage plan in our culture.

> Genesis 3:17-19 – Then to Adam He said, "Because you have listened to the voice of your wife, and have eaten from the tree about which I commanded you, saying, 'You shall not eat from it'; Cursed is the ground because of you; In toil you shall eat of it All the days of your life. [18] "Both thorns and thistles it shall grow for you; And you shall eat the plants of the field; [19] By the sweat of your face You shall eat bread, Till you return to the ground, Because from it you were taken; For you are dust, And to dust you shall return."

Think of that statement, "Because you have listened to the voice of your wife, . . ." What is the Lord saying to Adam? Could it be a possibility that Adam was not exercising his duty to be the spiritual leader of his marriage and subsequent family even at this early date? He had received the command from God – to not eat from this tree along with his wife, Eve, correct? Keep in mind that work is not the punishment here. After all, Adam was told to help in tending and working in the Garden of Eden while he was there as well. The curse was in the toil, sweat, and working amongst the thorns which made the once beautiful and invigorating work alongside his God to become the dreary and struggling work many are encumbered with today.

Adam and Eve may not have died physically the day they ate from the forbidden fruit, but they did die spiritually, and were separated from God. Thus all of us are born into sin. And we all will toil and sweat and work and eventually die physically as well. What will be the end results of the life we each live on this earth? Will each of us be reborn spiritually through Christ and bear fruit for Him? Be careful how you build. The results will either be long and lasting, or burnt up in a flash. Check out **1 Corinthians 3:10-15** for the description.

So we can see that the "MEN," as well as the women have contributed to our fallen sinful state. No one is absolved from blame. We are all sinners – each and every one of us whether we choose to believe it or not.

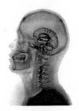

CHAPTER 3 – ARE

You "ARE" who you "ARE . . ." And so much of the time we don't really like who we "ARE". You might think to yourself, "why wasn't I born with all the gifts that guy possesses? Look at him, he's just cruisin' along with not a concern or problem in the world. He's got it made in the shade, man . . . and it's just not fair that I wasn't born as privileged as him." Or, "look at her. She's so beautiful and can attract any guy she wants; guys that will call and ask her out. She'll never have to worry about working and taking her kids to be raised by a day-care center. Or, "Oh my, look at their house!"

We all compare. We fantasize and daydream about how we've been so deprived and not gotten a fair shake like others have received. The New Testament book of James speaks to this.

> James 1:14-15 – But each one is tempted when he is carried away and enticed by his own lust. [15] Then when lust has conceived, it gives birth to sin; and when sin is accomplished, it brings forth death.

The sin nature is there to start with, which gives us the capacity to compare ourselves with others and have desires that start to formulate in our minds. Comparing and desires give way to envy and covetousness for what we see that others around us have, whether it be possessions, looks, or accolades from others – you name it, we desire it.

We want what *we* want so badly – what *we* feel *we* deserve that belongs to others while *we* don't even consider that *we* are so much better off than most of those around us in the world. It's uncanny the tendency we have to compare ourselves with those who are more prosperous than we are, and never with those who are less fortunate. It is our inherent sin nature. It is our lust for what others have that runs before our eyes and in our minds. Whether it be on TV, the internet, at home, work, or play, we want it.

Have you ever noticed this? We don't want to be whatever, or wherever we are either. It's that old, "the grass is always greener on the other side" malady, that we all struggle with. We keep telling ourselves, "I'll be happy when . . ." It starts early in life and goes on into old age. We keep telling ourselves . . . I'll be happy when . . . I lose my first tooth . . . or . . .

I'll be happy when . . . I get braces on my teeth . . . or . . .

I'll be happy when . . . I get my first boyfriend . . . or . . .

I'll be happy when . . . I get my driver's license . . . or . . .

I'll be happy when . . . I graduate from high school . . . or . . .

I'll be happy when . . . I graduate from college . . . or . . .

I'll be happy when . . . I get married . . . or . . .

I'll be happy when . . . I have my first child . . . or . . .

I'll be happy when . . . I get the kids out of the house . . . or . . .

I'll be happy when . . . I get that promotion and increased pay . . . or . . .

I'll be happy when . . . I get those grandkids . . . or . . .

I'll be happy when . . . I retire . . . or . . . or . . . or . . .

You get the picture. We go through our brief lives looking for happiness, and never get to a point of having that happiness. Listen to what Jesus says . . . He knows what true happiness is . . .

Matthew 25:21 – "His master said to him, 'Well done, good and faithful slave; you were faithful with a few things, I will put you in charge of many things, enter into the joy of your master.'

John 10:10 – "The thief comes only to steal, and kill, and destroy; I came that they might have life, and might have *it* abundantly.

Our sinful desires want to rob us of true happiness, which can only be realized in a relationship with our Savior, and then extend out to those He brings us into contact with. Those desires, as well as Satan, want to destroy us and all those around us. They appear so very enticing and beautiful . . . all the while those wants draw us to death and destruction. It even happened in Moses' day . . .

Leviticus 18:1-5 – Then the LORD spoke to Moses, saying, ² "Speak to the sons of Israel and say to them, 'I am the LORD your God. ³ 'You shall not do what is done in the land of Egypt where you lived, nor are you to do what is done in the land of Canaan where I am bringing you; you shall not walk in their statutes. ⁴ 'You

**are to perform My judgments and keep My statutes, to
live in accord with them; I am the LORD your God.
⁵ 'So you shall keep My statutes and My judgments, by
which a man may live if he does them; I am the LORD.**

God warned Moses and those following him to cling to His
statutes and not have desires for what those around them were
doing. This goes for us as well and makes for hard decisions
and difficult circumstances for all of us who are trying to grow
closer to Christ and be in His will, living by the power of His
Holy Spirit. God tells Moses, as well as us, that we are to keep
His statutes and judgments, by which we may live . . . if we will
do so. How are we doing with this command from our God?

Not so well, I'm afraid. I've read and observed that we all
are drawn to what keeps our attention. Whatever keeps our
attention and draws our focus the most is going to dictate
what we are thinking about. It also determines what we are
striving after. Have you ever thought about that? I think most
of us haven't even considered this concept of why we do what
we do each day. We just do it, and go on and do it the next day
and the next.

I need to interject an unofficial survey that I have
conducted at least a dozen times at five different churches,
in two denominations, amongst those who regularly attend
church and Sunday school . . .

I hand out small squares of paper to each of the participants
and ask them for only two numbers to be placed on the
paper – one at the top . . . and one at the bottom. (No names
please.) In fact, I'm going to ask you to do this in your mind
or on a piece of paper right now as well...

For your top number – How many minutes average per
day for the last seven days . . . have you spent in reverential,
solitudinal prayer? (Don't include praying before meals, or

while driving, walking, running, etc. – For this survey, I'm talking about prayer on your knees or at a regular spot in your home and your only concern or focus is spending time before your God and Savior . . . in prayer to Him!) Got it?

For your second number – How many minutes average per day for the last seven days . . . have you spent reading from God's Word – the Bible? (Don't include devotional books, Bible verse of the day emails, etc. – For this survey, I'm talking about reading from God's instruction Book to us . . . the Bible!) Got it?

Here's the deal . . . I have a good idea what your numbers are. I've seen the results too many times in too many groups! In regular church attendees these two numbers are virtually non-existent. Most papers come back 1/0 – 0/0 – 2/0 – 1/2 – or the occasional 5/10 – and the very rare 30/45. The absolute best result I've ever gotten was a month ago from a Sunday school class where the average numbers for the class were 12 minutes in prayer and 23 minutes reading their Bible each day – I was blown away!

What does this unofficial survey tell us? My thinking is that we don't spend time in relationship, focus, and prayer with the Savior we say we worship. We "mouth the words" that we love Him, but don't follow through with showing Him our love by spending time with Him in prayer and His Word. Read **John 14** and Jesus Himself speaks to us about our love of Him resulting in our "obeying His Word". Thus, we have no training up of our minds by Him and His Word . . . so we end up not devoting any of our attention to Jesus Christ and His will for our lives. Instead, we devote our attention to the world and what it would have us think about . . . all of which is actually of Satan.

Listen up! You end up being what you are thinking about! Those envious and covetous thoughts don't bring the things we are coveting, they bring the black and deceitful heart of sinful discontent described in **Jeremiah 17:9**. Those seemingly happy desires we want and crave don't bring those desires any closer; they only bring broken lives and broken longings for wrongful and deceptive things that we think will make us happy. Want proof? Look at the last house, car, TV, jewelry, or computer you bought. My son Joseph and I were driving down the Interstate a couple of weeks ago; the highway that goes smack-dab down the middle of the town we live in. I said, "Have you ever thought about this? That each and every one of these cars, trucks, and other vehicles travelling around us was brand-spanking new at one time, without a scratch, dent, or flaw in the shiny new paint job." Joseph responded that he, in fact, had thought about that as well. So, how do you feel about that new car after you've had it for five to ten years? What about the house? It needs repairs, and while you're thinking about it, it doesn't have the "up-to-date" floor plan that your best friend's new house has. The TV is outdated, the computer is too slow, and you've noticed nicer, more expensive jewelry that now has your attention.

My point is we long for what has our attention and for most of us, that attention is on the short-term, the fleeting, and the truly meaningless. All this stuff is going to be burnt-up and gone my friend – long gone in just a few years. Wouldn't we, and those around us be better served if we had our attention devoted to the eternity that each of us are going to end up in? After all, each one of us will be in one of two places – either in heaven or hell . . . that's it. A Pastor stated that he was on a mission trip to the Philippines when a woman came up to him and said, "You Americans . . . you are choking on all your blessings!" Food for thought don't you agree?

Matthew 13:22 – "And the one on whom seed was sown among the thorns, this is the man who hears the word, and the worry of the world, and the deceitfulness of riches choke the word, and it becomes unfruitful.

1 John 2:15-17 – Do not love the world, nor the things in the world. If anyone loves the world, the love of the Father is not in him. [16] For all that is in the world, the lust of the flesh and the lust of the eyes and the boastful pride of life, is not from the Father, but is from the world. [17] And the world is passing away, and also its lusts; but the one who does the will of God abides forever.

So if we know that these new toys eventually fade, and if we know we will each spend eternity in one of two places, how can we change what has our attention? The number one thing we can do is pray and ask our Savior to help us to "die to ourselves" and look to Him. Now that is a novel idea! If we don't like who we are, or where we find ourselves, most likely we are the ones who have made the decisions that have gotten us to this juncture. Do we think and trust that God may have a better plan and purpose for our lives than we could even dream of? Actually He does. He wants us to earnestly seek Him above all else. You know why? Because He alone is worthy of seeking! All other things are false gods and idols which will fade and go away. Jesus Christ alone is worthy of our seeking Him out and worshipping Him. And when we diligently and intently seek Him, then and only then will we find the true happiness and significant purpose that He has in store for us as we grow in our faith in and our relationship with Him.

James 1:25 – But one who looks intently at the perfect law, the *law* of liberty, and abides by it, not having

become a forgetful hearer but an effectual doer, this man shall be blessed in what he does.

The effort to get rid of the tyrannies of "busy-ness" so rampant around each of us is truly worth it. You know as well as I do, that you can only maintain relationships with those that you give your attention to. Do you want to really have a closer relationship with our Savior? Then do what a mentor told me some thirty years ago . . ." Mark, there is no "try" because "try" will never get anything meaningful accomplished. There is only "do!" If you make up your mind that you're not going to "try" to have that closer relationship with Christ . . . but that you are going to "do" it instead, just watch and see how He will respond and draw you ever nearer to Himself with an intimacy you never dreamed you could have with our God and Savior. Give Him ten to fifteen minutes of uninterrupted quiet-time in prayer and reading His Word each morning and MAKE it THE priority of your entire day. If you do this, just wait and watch as that 10-15 minutes each morning turns into thirty, and then forty five, and then sixty minutes with Him. What you will find is that you will so look forward to your morning time with Jesus Christ, you won't need that snooze button . . . or even the alarm for that matter.

Look at these verses which may help you to divert your attention to the One who deserves it . . .

Hebrews 11:6 – And without faith it is impossible to please *Him*, for he who comes to God must believe that He is, and *that* He is a rewarder of those who seek Him.

Joshua 1:7-9 – "Only be strong and very courageous; be careful to do according to all the law which Moses

My servant commanded you; do not turn from it to the right or to the left, so that you may have success wherever you go. [8] "This book of the law shall not depart from your mouth, but you shall meditate on it day and night, so that you may be careful to do according to all that is written in it; for then you will make your way prosperous, and then you will have success. [9] "Have I not commanded you? Be strong and courageous! Do not tremble or be dismayed, for the LORD your God is with you wherever you go."

Jeremiah 29:11-13 – 'For I know the plans that I have for you,' declares the LORD, 'plans for welfare and not for calamity to give you a future and a hope. [12] 'Then you will call upon Me and come and pray to Me, and I will listen to you. [13] 'And you will seek Me and find *Me*, when you search for Me with all your heart.

Attention is something that we do have some control over. We can exercise control over what we spend our time pursuing. We can make a determined effort to come into Christ's presence each morning. Or, we can continue down the same weak and listless path of lukewarm faith we have been pursuing for all of our previous life. Why not start anew, and devote our time and efforts to our Lord and Savior Jesus Christ? Transformation is what we need. To be transformed more and more into the likeness and Spirit of Jesus Christ our Lord. More of Jesus and His Holy Spirit, and less of ourselves and self-centeredness. This is what we need more than anything.

Romans 12:1-2 – I urge you therefore, brethren, by the mercies of God, to present your bodies a

living and holy sacrifice, acceptable to God, *which is* your spiritual service of worship. ² And do not be conformed to this world, but be transformed by the renewing of your mind, that you may prove what the will of God is, that which is good and acceptable and perfect.

I've told my kids repeatedly, "Be careful of the friends you pick. Chances are, you'll become like them." This is true is it not? Whoever, or whatever we spend time with, we become like. Hence, the more time we spend with those drinking buddies the more alcohol we consume. The more time we spend with that girlfriend with the shopping obsession, the more we run up our credit card bill. Let me get a little more personal. Is your friend the alcohol you drink every night, or even throughout the day? How about pornography; is your time in seeming solitude spent in communion with the sick and perverse images and videos that you just can't seem to get out of your mind? A vast number of families struggle with these two maladies at the core of the problem in some manner, and they are wreaking havoc on those addicted to them! If either of these are your nemesis – RUN! RUN from them as fast as you can – and reach out to your Savior! You have picked the wrong friends to hang out with and they will destroy you and your family! The more time we occupy ourselves with the meaningless "tyrannies" around us the more we feel there is no real purpose for our lives.

God longs for us to long for Him, but He won't force Himself on us. If we truly don't want anything to do with God . . . instead of waiting for us to come to Him, He may eventually leave us to ourselves. God, through His Son, provides the redemption and reconciliation of His Son's shed blood on the Cross for payment for our sins, but He doesn't force us to receive that payment. We have to come to Christ in faith and avail ourselves to Him in submission and relationship in order to receive the Holy Spirit He has sent to indwell us. But again, we need to be careful how we respond to God's love and grace – we do have a choice and our true heart will be revealed eventually.

> **Ezekiel 14:7-8 – "For anyone of the house of Israel or of the immigrants who stay in Israel who separates himself from Me, sets up his idols in his heart, puts right before his face the stumbling block of his iniquity, and *then* comes to the prophet to inquire of Me for himself, I the LORD will be brought to answer him in My own person. ⁸ "And I shall set My face against that man and make him a sign and a proverb, and I shall cut him off from among My people. So you will know that I am the LORD.**

I've had it happen repeatedly in my office . . . an individual in meltdown-mode with tears streaming down his or her face, sobbing about where they are in life. The problem is that by all the standards the world would set, they should be the happiest person on the planet. They've either got a great company they own or work for, with plenty of income, or they've sold their company and are retired with no financial worries whatsoever. The common thread is that they are unhappy. The money didn't buy them the happiness they thought it would and sometimes has even become a burden to them. They feel they have no real purpose in this life and that those around them don't really love them for who they are, but only love them because they have the money.

If you truly want to find out who you "ARE" – go to God's Word . . .

Hebrews 4:12 – For the word of God is living and active and sharper than any two-edged sword, and piercing as far as the division of soul and spirit, of both joints and marrow, and able to judge the thoughts and intentions of the heart.

So if you don't like who you "ARE" or where you find yourself in life, remember this: you have had a part in where you've gotten. In fact, you have had a major part. Do you trust in yourself to get out of the predicament you find yourself in? Or will you go to the only One Who can absolutely help you no matter who or where you "ARE?"

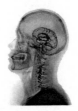

CHAPTER 4 – IDIOTS

What is your definition of an "IDIOT?" Some would say he's a fool. Others would say that he is just slow, and still others would say the world is full of them. And "idiots" may include both men and women you can be sure. I had a mentor tell me one time, "You know Mark, the world is full of idiots – and many of them are highly educated derelicts." It could and should be said, that there are a lot of people in this world who are too smart in their own eyes and too smart for their own good. We see them all the time, and I have to admit that sometimes the biggest one I see is the one I see in the mirror each morning. It's sad, but if we were all really honest with ourselves we each could say that we've occupied this pariah of positions.

Well, let me give you another definition of the word idiot . . .

"IDIOT"; a guy named Mark Peters! (I've even had people ask me if the x-ray on the cover of this book is of me!)

Let me explain . . . and please know that I rue this act, and am totally ashamed to have to share it with you.

It was just a few years after my first year-and-a-half long marriage that ended in divorce. Keyea and I had dated a while, and we decided to get married, and our wedding was down in

Houston at a nice small church in the West University area. After we exchanged our vows, we walked down the aisle, out of the church, and back up the side of the church on the concrete sidewalk. About midway up the sidewalk, yours truly, stopped and took my beautiful new bride by the arm and turned her to where she was facing me. It was then that I proceeded to say these words that absolutely haunt me to this very day . . .

I told Keyea, "You'd better be good to me!"

All I can say is that I thank the Lord that she didn't pack up and leave me right there on the spot! It is actually what probably should have happened, but somehow she stayed with me in spite of my being the epitome of an idiot!

My self-centeredness was my total focus. I was all about me, and still am at times, frankly. Have you ever felt that way about yourself? I've had to face it: I was an idiot extraordinaire at this moment. Guess what? I've gotta million of 'em I could share with you, but you don't have time . . . and I don't have the stomach to share with you all the senseless acts I've done! In the last chapter we discussed that whatever gets our attention is what drives us. For most of us it's ourselves that get that nod and "tip of the cap" as to where that attention is placed. We consider ourselves wise, and there is no doubt about it. What if we took the time out of our busy schedules and took a peek at what our God says about our puffing ourselves up? In the remainder of this chapter are a couple of excerpts from His Word for us to consider.

Hosea 4:6 – My people are destroyed for lack of knowledge. Because you have rejected knowledge, I also will reject you from being My priest. Since you have forgotten the law of your God, I also will forget your children.

Ouch! It kind of stings doesn't it? Keep in mind that God is talking about forgetting the law of God – His Word. As Forrest Gump used to say, "Stupid is as stupid does." My wife and I always told our kids to never use the word "stupid." They grew up thinking it was a really bad word, and it is. The trouble is that it fits with so many of us. While most of us don't think this word pertains to us, it is obvious that it does because of the questionable decisions we make when it comes to our families. It also applies to our decision to ignore and disdain the instruction book that our God gives us so that we might learn more about Him, as well as ourselves. Instead of looking to, and trusting God's Word, we entrust our family to the reality shows, the social media, and the instruction of anyone and anything out there under the Sun. It makes one wonder how many people in our churches are truly being saved, or instead, are on their way to perishing because they are lying to themselves about their walk of faith in Christ.

Listen to God's admonition to us in His Word . . .

2 Timothy 3:16-17 – All Scripture is inspired by God and profitable for teaching, for reproof, for correction, for training in righteousness; [17] that the man of God may be adequate, equipped for every good work.

I had an interesting conversation with the Principal of a 5A high school located in East Texas yesterday. He is a Christian also, and he and I were discussing the plight of our families. Mike informed me that he looked through the roles of his school a couple of months ago and was surprised to find that 52% of his students on the list who attended, had different last names than their present parents. That means over half of his kids enrolled were in blended, or divorced and remarried households. He said the number is actually larger because some of those with the same last name are now in a single parent household. It's just that their parent has not remarried – yet. I mentioned that there are a lot of kids who don't know what a basically normal family looks like because they've never seen one. They have no model of what a loving father or mother looks like because they have never had one.

Mike said, "It's funny you should mention role-models of parents for their kids, Mark." He then made another comment that I hadn't thought of specifically. He said, "There are a lot of 'throw-away' kids out there."

"What do you mean?" I asked.

Mike said, "The parents know they'll get jail-time if they abuse the kids while they're little, so they just wait until they are in the teenage years, and then they abandon them and pretty much have them fend for themselves, though they're still living at home."

"What? Are you serious?" I asked.

"It's rampant, Mark! I see it all the time. The kid may still be in the house but in essence they are all on their own." Then I thought of one of my younger friends who had told me that this is the way he actually grew up. His parents divorced. His Dad moved away, and his Mom had a job that she didn't get off from until about 12:00 at night – every night. He said from the time he was twelve years old, there was no one home when he got home each and every day. And that he was basically on his own from twelve years of age on. How sad for these kids. They grow up basically fending for themselves and sometimes end up being parents to their parents, at least some of them.

These kids are essentially sacrificed on the altar of needy parents who are in need of parents they may never have had either. This need for parental attention crosses all economic and social strata's. I even heard of a family who bought their 16 year-old daughter her own house – just to get her out of their house. It sets up a vicious cycle that seems to repeat itself over and over. There's another altar of sacrifice that families are offered up on and it's at the other end of the spectrum.

It is definitely not a lack of attention, but can be just as insidious. This altar of sacrifice is the altar of organized sports for our kids. I've had several friends who have shared with me that they wish they would have known how this was going to turn out years ago when they started. It started out so innocent, so benign at the beginning. Their kid was a little, or maybe even significantly better than the other kids on his baseball, soccer, or basketball team. He showed so much promise, that the coach told his parents he needed to be on a select team to hone his skills even further. Then on top of the select team tournaments, the "skills camps" for speed, endurance, and technique training was recommended. All of this was done in hopes that their kid would "make it big" – and get that prized scholarship to a college to play a sport and who knows . . . maybe even become a professional in their prized arena.

And yet another family sacrificed for the glory of sport. Why do I say sacrificed? Because I get calls from those same friends asking me how they can get their young adult kids in college (without the coveted scholarship I might add!) to re-engage in their walk of faith with Jesus Christ. They used to go to church and their kids were so devoted to their walk of faith early on. But that was before they quit going to church in order to go to the swim meets, soccer, baseball, or basketball tournaments that took them away from consistently worshipping their Lord and Savior with the family. Now their kids are away from home and not really interested in going to church anymore. It just doesn't seem that important to them now. And who really believes all that "Jonah in the belly of the great fish" stuff anyway?

Therefore we have another generation growing away from Christ and His Holy Word. All those Bible stories they learned as kids become just that – "stories". In fact, they just don't really believe all that gibberish anymore at all! They're in college now and so much smarter than they used to be when they believed all that stuff. And besides, their professors and teachers at their universities don't believe in all that "living water" mumbo jumbo either. It is just foolishness to them . . .

> **1 Corinthians 1:18-21 – For the word of the cross is to those who are perishing foolishness, but to us who are being saved it is the power of God. [19] For it is written, "I will destroy the wisdom of the wise, And the cleverness of the clever I will set aside." [20] Where is the wise man? Where is the scribe? Where is the debater of this age? Has not God made foolish the wisdom of the world? [21] For since in the wisdom of God the world through its wisdom did not *come to* know God, God was well-pleased through the foolishness of the message preached to save those who believe.**

"It's just too easy!" say many. Unbelievers say "it's too easy" for them to receive and believe in Jesus Christ as their atoning sacrifice and be saved from sin and death. Do you know what? They're absolutely right! It is easy for them . . . but guess who had to do the hard part? No it wasn't easy for the saving atonement and grace and sacrifice that Jesus, God the Father's Son, provided for all of us sinners. It was the biggest price ever paid in the cosmos for anything! And guess what, He alone could live the perfectly sinless life to impute that life to us, while shedding His blood on the cross to pay for the countless sins each of us impute to Him while we live on this earth. There is a huge misconception by most people out there of what the true gospel message is. Many think Jesus was just a good man or a prophet, and that He was meek and weak, as well as not being assertive enough. They fail to see Jesus for Who He actually was . . . God on earth, the obedient Son to the Holy Father, and the loving Savior who is our only hope as the sinners we are. Jesus paid an incalculable price for all of us on this earth who claim Him as our Lord. He paid the price for those who refuse His gift as well, so the gift goes unclaimed and unredeemed. Refused and unwanted, His gift of grace and forgiveness stands there for all to see, yet it is still rejected by some. Many who do reject Christ are so very wise in their own eyes.

1 Corinthians 1:25-29 – Because the foolishness of God is wiser than men, and the weakness of God is stronger than men. [26] For consider your calling, brethren, that there were not many wise according to the flesh, not many mighty, not many noble; [27] but God has chosen the foolish things of the world to shame the wise, and God has chosen the weak things of the world to shame the things which are strong, [28] and the base things of the world and the despised, God has chosen, the things that are not, that He might nullify the things that are, [29] that no man should boast before God.

Do you think it's possible that we have spent considerable time trying to "get ahead" and go for broke at being "book smart" – while remaining devoid of taking in our Father's Word and receiving true wisdom from Him instead? There is a huge and incomparable difference between being smart and being wise.

I had a patient who was a brilliant and smart man. He retired from a big company with a nice, fat nest-egg for his retirement. He then went on to get his CFP (Certified Financial Planner) license in order to make sure he could maintain and even grow that nest-egg. The problem was he was diagnosed with cancer and he knew his time was short. Being one of the nicest men you'd ever want to meet, it was heartbreaking to hear what a mutual friend of ours told me after this gentleman succumbed to his cancer. Our friend told me that they had gone to lunch one day a few months before he passed, and this was what he shared with him. The man said, "You know Jack, I had it all figured out. I worked hard, made plenty of money, and didn't squander it away. That lump sum of stocks, bonds, and cash was what I had devoted my entire life to and I had achieved my goals. But do you know what troubles me the most, now that I know I've got just a short time left on this earth? I don't think in all my life that I've ever led even one person to my Lord & Savior Jesus Christ. I feel like I've wasted my entire life!" How sad to have spent one's whole life seeking what the world told him would bring him lasting happiness only to find that the lasting and eternal happiness he longed for at his death was on an entirely different road.

What a place to be when you're at the end of your life and all is said and done. This man was absolutely a Christian. He was a very good, and smart man too. But he may not have been wise. He certainly wasn't as wise as he should have been when it came to sharing his faith . . . even in his own estimation. This lack of wisdom spills over to all areas of our lives. We've set our eyes on the wrong goals, the wrong priorities, and the wrong meaning of what true happiness is.

This lack of wisdom and misguided quest for what the world and Satan say will make us happy is the source of much of the breakdown of our marriages and families as well. Our eyes are off of our Savior and what He wants our families to end up being.

On the other hand our eyes are on what the world is constantly telling us to do . . . TAKE CARE OF YOURSELF! There is probably not a week that goes by that either in my practice or in visiting with people in the community, I don't hear or see the ravages of divorce on the rampage. It is either acquaintances I can't believe are in the midst of getting a divorce, or a friend/patient talking of how their marriage is in trouble. It ranges from, "I've had a long-term problem with alcohol Doc . . ." or "My wife tells me she's having more fun with her divorced friends than with me and the kids . . ." You name it, people are looking for love in all the wrong places, and never finding true love. Then the family is out the window and the whole never-ending cycle of broken families is carried on to the next generation because there was no good foundation or example set for their kids to emulate. It is so very prevalent that the wisdom we all need is not there in the decisions we make and the havoc wreaked is enormous.

At some point, we need to face the undeniable truth that there is no wisdom in this world that compares with the Wisdom of the God of the universe. He points it out to us over and over in His Holy Word . . .

Proverbs 1:7 – The fear of the LORD is the beginning of knowledge; Fools despise wisdom and instruction.

Proverbs 14:16 – A wise man is cautious and turns away from evil, But a fool is arrogant and careless.

Proverbs 17:24 – Wisdom is in the presence of the one who has understanding, But the eyes of a fool are on the ends of the earth.

Proverbs 18:2 – A fool does not delight in understanding, But only in revealing his own mind.

Proverbs 26:12 – Do you see a man wise in his own eyes? There is more hope for a fool than for him.

However Satan would have us believe that we are wise. He lurks around like a roaring lion seeking to devour all the misled and "wise" people he can. The truth is, he is the king of the idiots and the father of lies. **Matthew 7:13-27** speaks of two paths, two gates, two prophets, two fruits, two trees, two men, two houses, two foundations, which each lead to two final destinations . . . only two. One road leads to heaven and the other to hell and there is no in-between amongst the two. Which God shares with us in His Word . . .

John 3:18-21 – "He who believes in Him is not judged; he who does not believe has been judged already, because he has not believed in the name of the only begotten Son of God. [19] "And this is the judgment, that the light is come into the world, and men loved the darkness rather than the light; for their deeds were evil. [20] "For everyone who does evil hates the light, and does not come to the light, lest his deeds should be exposed. [21] "But he who practices the truth comes to the light, that his deeds may be manifested as having been wrought in God."

John 3:36 – "He who believes in the Son has eternal life; but he who does not obey the Son shall not see life, but the wrath of God abides on him."

Matthew 25:46 – "And these will go away into eternal punishment, but the righteous into eternal life."

2 Thessalonians 2:8-12 – And then that lawless one will be revealed whom the Lord will slay with the breath of His mouth and bring to an end by the appearance of His coming; *9 that is,* the one whose coming is in accord with the activity of Satan, with all power and signs and false wonders, *10* and with all the deception of wickedness for those who perish, because they did not receive the love of the truth so as to be saved. *11* And for this reason God will send upon them a deluding influence so that they might believe what is false, *12* in order that they all may be judged who did not believe the truth, but took pleasure in wickedness.

We could go on and on with Scriptures describing the differences of these two ends. Wisdom vs. foolishness, and heaven vs. hell. Those who discount the Word of God aren't going to believe what these verses say anyway. Their minds are made up and their decision is made . . . or is it? The Lord can prick the heart of even the most ardent and zealous unbeliever and turn that stone-cold heart into a soft, pliable and loving one. So keep praying for your family and friends. God the Father, Jesus the Son, and the Holy Spirit can even change the "IDIOTS" and help them to not be, "Stupid is as stupid does."

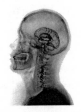

CHAPTER 5 – !

Everyone is SO "EMPHATIC!!!" Have you noticed? It's flourishing, overt and everywhere. All are seeking to make their mark, no matter how degrading or meaningless it is. Give them some attention on a video or in print and they are totally – ON IT! It is as if there is no limit to what people will do to have their five minutes of fame. Can you think of anyone on a grander scale than the original sinner that started out the same way? How about the king of this world for this time right now, Satan himself. He went for the gusto and grabbed all he could, even reaching for equality with God Himself. Big mistake, it couldn't happen. He overreached and lost what could have been a wonderful life of eternity with his Father.

You could bring this down to our own level as well. We see the overreach around us and have gotten more and more lax in using our judgment to discern what is right and what is wrong. Take a few minutes and read these next few passages and then reread them for yourself. Does this sound familiar to what you see going on day to day around your world?

2 Timothy 3:1-9 – But realize this, that in the last days difficult times will come. ² For men will be lovers of

self, lovers of money, boastful, arrogant, revilers, disobedient to parents, ungrateful, unholy, [3] unloving, irreconcilable, malicious gossips, without self-control, brutal, haters of good, [4] treacherous, reckless, conceited, lovers of pleasure rather than lovers of God; [5] holding to a form of godliness, although they have denied its power; and avoid such men as these. [6] For among them are those who enter into households and captivate weak women weighed down with sins, led on by various impulses, [7] always learning and never able to come to the knowledge of the truth. [8] And just as Jannes and Jambres opposed Moses, so these *men* also oppose the truth, men of depraved mind, rejected as regards the faith. [9] But they will not make further progress; for their folly will be obvious to all, as also that of those *two* came to be.

One thing that doesn't appear to be the case is that of the last verse in this segment of Scripture. It does seem that people these days are making further progress even though their folly is obvious to everyone. And the lies they are propagating are creating a tremendous assault being waged on the family not only in our country but around the world. Satan is loosening all the stops at his disposal in order to bring the family unit to its knees and cutting the legs out from under it. There is no definition of what a normal or stand-up family looks like, much less, a God-fearing family. The breakdown is not only going quickly, it is going "viral" – with the internet as the conduit to help the speedy demise. Overload is the weapon, and our focus on the truth is the dying and crumbling foundation that is teetering on the brink.

If the previous verses didn't get your dander stirred up and swirling around, how about these at the end of **Romans 1** . . .

Romans 1:28-32 – And just as they did not see fit to acknowledge God any longer, God gave them over to a depraved mind, to do those things which are not proper, [29] being filled with all unrighteousness, wickedness, greed, evil; full of envy, murder, strife, deceit, malice; *they are* gossips, [30] slanderers, haters of God, insolent, arrogant, boastful, inventors of evil, disobedient to parents, [31] without understanding, untrustworthy, unloving, unmerciful; [32] and, although they know the ordinance of God, that those who practice such things are worthy of death, they not only do the same, but also give hearty approval to those who practice them.

This is US my friend! We have seen the enemy... and THEY IS US! It is so very obvious and right in front of our noses, yet we don't stand up and even say one word to denounce the wickedness we see around us. It appears we are actually growing more and more numb to the sin that is so prevalent in our world. A common thread in these two segments of Scriptures is the commentary on the family unit which jumps off the page. It is the fact that the kids disobey their parents. Might that be because their parents are not around anymore, or that they've been divorced multiple times?

Keeping our marriages together much less our families, is getting harder and harder. How is it that those who desire to have a God honoring family, seem to now be the ones in the minority of those families out there? We go along with the herd trying to cull our family out of the massive sea of the broken family wasteland that is so widespread around us. We wall our kids off in private schools or better yet – we homeschool our kids. Yeah, that'll do it. We didn't used to have to think along these terms – separating our kids from other kids and in some people's opinion, wrongful teaching. All of our kids are hugely impacted by both of the parents they are raised by, even if the parents are divorced. It seems that the breakdown of the family unit is becoming so extensive however, that many of the kids have no clear vision of what a "normal" family looks like. The families portrayed on the tube are so vastly different from what the "Father Knows Best" and "Leave it to Beaver" programs portrayed a few decades ago. Our media elite are hell-bent on redefining the family in the most outrageous scenarios possible in order to glean better ratings and make more money. They emphasize bizarre, and even grotesque relationships that would have actually shocked us twenty to thirty years ago. Yet now, they are accepted not only as possible, but really plausible.

The emphasis on the Dad is that he is an idiot and lost without the woman who directs him – no matter what their relationship is. A strong Dad, who leads his family and "knows the program" is obsolete. Think about this, that strong Dad in our families is growing more obsolete as well. Our kids don't see on TV, much less at home, a father who loves his wife and treats her with respect as his cherished soul-mate. They don't see a loving Dad that holds his kids accountable and expects respect from them while also showing compassion and love to his kids. It's just not out there folks! At least in large numbers. And who's to blame? We can't play the victim forever . . . we don't have anyone to blame but ourselves. We have succumbed to the values and morals of the world around us, instead of clinging to God and His plan. We've let the world dictate what we will watch on TV. We have stood idly by, and let our kids train us up, rather than us training them up. In an effort to get on the good side of our kids, we parents have allowed them to demand that we obey them . . . just so they'll give us a little attention and approval. Instead of Mom staying home and helping to raise and teach the kids, she is out in the workforce in order to have the nicer car or the bigger home. In the same vein, Dad is putting in his ten to twelve hour days, or flying out of town for two to four days per week – every week. The day-care centers raise herds of kids with no telling what kind of values and life-lessons learned in the chaos of each day of abandoned kids. We ignore God's instruction book and what He tells us about parenting in it . . .

> Deuteronomy 6:4-7 – "Hear, O Israel! The LORD is our God, the LORD is one! 5 "And you shall love the LORD your God with all your heart and with all your soul and with all your might. 6 "And these words, which I am commanding you today, shall be on your heart; 7 and you shall teach them diligently to your sons and shall talk of them when you sit in your house and when you walk by the way and when you lie down and when you rise up.

> Proverbs 22:6 – Train up a child in the way he should go, Even when he is old he will not depart from it.

Look around at your family. Don't worry, to a certain degree we are all dysfunctional – even the best of families. That's because we are broken and fallen sinners, and will be until we're called to our final home in heaven . . . unless we remain condemned as eternal sinners in hell. Go to my first book and read it if you want some ideas in how to avoid the torment.

I had breakfast with a good friend last week and he is earnestly seeking out Jesus Christ in his life. He and his wife are both involved in Bible Study Fellowship and are expecting their first child in a few months. I mentioned to him that there are two things that Keyea and I wouldn't change about the way we've brought up our kids.

The first decision that we made was that Keyea would stay at home with Kailey after she was born, so she quit her teaching job at Conroe High School that summer. I know this is harder for some to accomplish than others as there are many more women who are not electing to stay home with the kids. Some couples might find it a harder burden to bear in losing an income in order to sustain their standard of living. This was the case with my friend that morning. He told me, "Mark, at least at 'this five seconds' in our lives, my wife and I can't possibly have her quit her job. She has a very nice income and we simply cannot stay in the house we are in and live in the manner we are presently living without that income."

"I understand that . . ." I replied, "but just understand that 'this five seconds' turns into 'another five seconds' and then before you know it, the kids are gone.

At some point we all must make hard decisions. Have you ever noticed that when you tell yourself that "it can't be done," oftentimes you are forced into a tight spot and that inevitable scenario gets played-out, whether you want it to be played-out or not? Once you're on the other side, you realize, "Hey . . . it can be done! In fact, it's already done! What was I so scared about?" I've seen this for Keyea and me multiple times through our marriage. It happened when we decided to give our church more than we thought we could possibly afford thirty years ago. We're still giving and though we might have had a little more in our retirement account now, that was not our money anyway. It's the Lord's money, and by giving it back to Him, He gave us discipline to not live above our means, and he's blessed us all the same. Keyea staying at home with the kids has reaped way, way more benefits than we could have possibly gotten from her keeping on working to make some more money and taking the kids to daycare. WE raised our kids, not some Aunt, Grandma, or daycare center. And don't misunderstand, we haven't been perfect parents, nor have we raised perfect kids, but at least at this juncture in our lives we can see that Keyea staying at home was best for our family.

Unfortunately for many, this is absolutely not an option to even consider. My hat is off to the single mothers out there who are working themselves to exhaustion each and every day. Their "ex" doesn't seem to be able to come up with the means to help support the kids he partook in bringing into this world, so she's left to fend for them all. This is yet another symptom of the ravages of divorce so prevalent in and around us today.

The second thing we wouldn't change is that we started our kids in BSF (Bible Study Fellowship) when they were each two years old. We have discovered that this was pivotal in helping us to raise our kids to have a strong faith in Jesus Christ. A Pastor who specializes in Youth Ministry came and spoke at our church several years back. He said that what the education and development gurus are saying is that kids have the majority of their world-view established by the time they are five years old! You got that? They've already had the majority of their views on their faith, on marriage, on society, and the world formed by the time they are five. WOW! Even more reason for Mom to be at home with them rather than farming them out to the daycare center.

Having Kailey and Joseph in BSF those early years has enabled our family to stay strong in our faith and carry it on out into the world around us in a meaningful way. Kailey found a great church home at Texas A&M on her own. She stayed consistent in her attendance and found a nice group of young adults who are strong in their faith as well. She even made friends with a wonderful couple who basically adopted all the kids who sat at their table in the Sunday School class for the time they were at college. Joseph, at seventeen, is actually helping to lead and facilitate a Bible study at his high school. And friends who are strong in their faith also surround him.

Joseph and I tend to end up going to the golf course to play 9 holes of golf when he or I want to visit with each other. We pretty much know that's the case, so it's not a competitive venture. I try to let him guide the discussion, but sometimes I too have concerns I feel I would like to discuss with him. A couple of weeks ago we were playing and having a discussion about dating, girl-friends, and the complexities of relationships. After about an hour of non-stop conversation of the pro's & con's of having a steady girlfriend or not, Joseph made a statement that stopped me in my tracks. He said, "You know Dad, I think this is a case where I just have to trust that you have been around longer than I have, and that you know what is best for me . . . so I think I'm gonna take your advice and do what you recommend in this situation." What a statement to hear coming from a 17 year old!

I admit, it doesn't always go that way, and sometimes my kids think I'm too old-fashioned in my ways, but by and large it does seem that they at least listen to me. Both of my kids are at way different places than I was at their age, and as I watch them I am both thankful . . . and humbled.

However sometimes we get a whack up the side of our head as I did this past week. Kailey and I went out on a date. She's just graduated from A&M and about to launch out into this great big world. We went to a restaurant and had a two hour conversation over dinner. It was very revealing to this loving and overprotective Dad. While I've always had the idea that both my kids are strong in their faith in Jesus

Christ, Kailey helped me to understand that she, in fact, has struggled with her faith, even as recently as this last semester of college.

She stated that she had actually felt that being a Christian is too hard at times, and that the pressure is always there. She felt sometimes she might even want to take a break from all the pressure of being perceived as a 'perfect' young lady, from a 'perfect' family. She knows too well that we, as a family, are not perfect, and have our own faults and sins to bear.

After taking a big sip of ice tea so I could regroup, do you know what I did? I said, "I'm sorry, Baby. I don't mean to put that pressure on you . . . I know you put enough of that on yourself."

And she does, just like most of our kids she not only has pressure put on her by the world she lives in, she puts tons of pressure on herself! She really, really . . . I mean really wants to make her Mom & Dad proud! I need to give her the space and room to be able to make her own mistakes though, and not place her on a pedestal that she can't possibly stay on top of. The Lord knows that I, a scumbag sinner myself, have skeletons in my closet that I hope and pray none of you ever find out about. Think about it. What if . . . each of us had a videotape of our thoughts played out for everyone on the earth to see . . . for just the last twenty four hours? We would all cringe at the thought.

I told her, "Kailey, I know you're not perfect and neither is our family, but one thing I am pretty sure of is this . . . you don't have as many scars and skeletons in your closet as I did when I was your age. It is a fine and tenuous line I walk as your Dad, trying to be an encourager to you on your walk of faith . . . and not be oppressively so. I'm going to ask the Lord to help me remove that burden of pressure from your shoulders, Baby."

Ladies and gentlemen, it's that "idiot/sinner" thing rearing its ugly head over and over in my own life. Here I am, thinking that I'm doing all I can to "train up" my daughter . . . only to realize that the pressure I've put on her may have nearly driven her away from our Savior! There is a balance, and we absolutely cannot maintain it on our own. That balance has to come from our Savior and His Holy Spirit. They alone can help us to strike the right balance. The trouble is . . . we don't seek their advice on how to do so. Keyea and I are so very thankful that the emphasis we have maintained the most for our family is our faith in Jesus Christ. We have tried to de-emphasize the material and sexual facets of our culture around us. We all know our kids will get plenty of that pushed down their throats. I have tried to emphasize Christ and His will, purpose and plan for their lives. I have seen others trying to push their kids into relationships with the opposite sex even as early as elementary school. I just don't understand why these parents would do that. Why put those kids in situations they're not ready to handle, increase their heartache when the relationship is broken off, and set them up for "mini-divorces" . . . that they may carry into their adult life as a way of life.

I've heard of Mothers trying to get their daughters to go on dates when they are in elementary school. Seriously? Or parents that take their twelve and thirteen year olds to New York City to shop for their wardrobe. Are you kidding? We are to be careful how we train our kids up in this life as they will carry, and often repeat the things that get our attention. They will then focus their attention on whatever we lead them to deem important. We are admonished in the Scriptures, at multiple places, to train up our kids. Don't try to grow your kids up too soon as many do. Give them the gift of a childhood free from the worries of being a grownup, obsessed with the stuff of this fallen world. Train them up in what will last this lifetime and on into eternity because if you don't the world will train them so rapidly that it will make your head spin. So be careful who is training your kids!

> Ephesians 6:1-4 – Children, obey your parents in the Lord, for this is right. [2] Honor your father and mother (which is the first commandment with a promise), [3] that it may be well with you, and that you may live long on the earth. [4] And, fathers, do not provoke your children to anger; but bring them up in the discipline and instruction of the Lord.

So, what are you "EMPHASIZING" in your life and for your kids? Is it the outrageous and emphatic that the world is obsessed with? Or the love of Christ? Chances are that you're reaping what you've sown over the years when it comes to your family. Do you want to change your emphasis in your family? Jesus Christ can help you to do so . . .

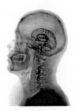

CHAPTER 6 – AND

There is a lot of angst, fear, "AND" trepidation out there. It's a general feeling that things just aren't quite right. There is an uneasiness in the air and a lot of people just can't seem to put their finger on what the problem is. I have patients who make comments in regard to this feeling frequently. Face it, people are anxious and worried about a lot of things these days. It's as if there are too many things to do and too many choices to make. Oftentimes the choices are not real clear as to what is truly the right thing to do. Why is this? In this fallen world Satan knows that one of the best things he can do to keep us away from our Lord and Savior is to keep us occupied with other things. Many of which are worries and fears. This sense of overload in our minds seemingly leaves us with no other choice than to try to stay ahead of the dire consequences we feel are just around the bend. They may be real and concrete, but many of them are simply figments of our imagination. They are always there, always lurking, always just out of reach to grasp and get rid of. However, these concerns occupy our thoughts to the extent that many of us are always just below the panic level, if not actually there.

What would you say if I told you that there is a reason for

this angst, fear, and trepidation and that there is a real cause? What would you do if the problem has been spelled out from long ago in ages past right before your nose? Read through the next few pages and maybe we can understand why we are so wound up.

> **Genesis 3:14-15 – And the LORD God said to the serpent, "Because you have done this, Cursed are you more than all cattle, And more than every beast of the field; On your belly shall you go, And dust shall you eat All the days of your life; ¹⁵ And I will put enmity Between you and the woman, And between your seed and her seed; He shall bruise you on the head, And you shall bruise him on the heel."**

You see we have an enemy and he is not happy. Satan has lost the war and can only seek to win skirmishes along the way to his crushing defeat and annihilation at the end times. Thus he loves his purpose – to make all of mankind miserable and doubting of their one true and holy God. Since he cannot be everywhere at once, Satan moves from place to place seeking to do as much damage as he possibly can to cause harm and mayhem for human kind. To cover more territory, he sends out his demons and minions to assist him in his endeavors. He knows that he only has so much time to exercise his forms of anarchy, so he makes hay while the opportunity is still in his grasp.

My friend, there is a battle going on and it is raging all around us. It is invisible, yet palpable, hidden, yet so evident. The battle I'm speaking of is the "Battle for our minds!" And though we are right in the midst of this battle, most of us have never even imagined that it is taking place, especially if we've never repented of our sin and asked Jesus Christ to be our

Lord and Savior. Even if we have received Christ, we probably haven't spent adequate time in His Word to be able to even know of this battle existing. Yes, I do think there is spiritual warfare going on all around us all the time. Do you? Many pooh-pooh and blow off the notion that there are clashes among the good and evil forces of the principalities of the air as stated in **Ephesians 6**. They do so at their own peril and danger.

The Israelites did the same and reaped what they sowed as revealed in the following passage:

> **Zechariah 11:15-16 – And the LORD said to me, "Take again for yourself the equipment of a foolish shepherd. [16] "For behold, I am going to raise up a shepherd in the land who will not care for the perishing, seek the scattered, heal the broken, or sustain the one standing, but will devour the flesh of the fat *sheep* and tear off their hoofs.**

I don't know about you, but I wouldn't relish having my hooves, or my feet torn off. The symbolism here is keen and intense, making one feel the agony of those affected by such savage and ravenous actions. There is no mercy here!

Let me ask you a question. Does this seem to be what you are seeing in the pain and heartache in the lives of many around you? Does it seem there is no rhyme or reason to the suffering going on in friends' lives, or in your own life for that matter? Here's the deal . . . we live in a fallen and sinful and broken world while this side of heaven . . . or hell! You pick your destination after reading about our Savior and the father of lies. It is the widest disparity between the two. But in this time and in this place, for right now, Satan has the upper hand and is tightening his grip on our world. It has already gotten ugly and will get much more so as time passes. The uneasiness and fear that occupies the minds of the masses of lost souls out there can and will get more horrid than it is even now. The information age and social media make for a hotbed of Satan exercising control over those whose minds are mush and open to his occupying of their beings through his minions. Just look at the bombardment of shootings, killings, human trafficking, fights over abortion, and the polarization of our planet earth. Yes, the lines are being drawn and the sides are being developed, for the war of the Cosmos! We, my friends, are currently in interesting times to be alive! The ramp-up of activity and discord, hatred and loathing, self-centeredness and greed make for a bad combination. It is like our entire world is walking along on the edge of the finest of razor-blades. One little slip or misstep will set in motion the beginning of the collapse of our nation, then the world, then all heck breaks loose. And once that downfall starts, get ready – the actions of people who are scared and desperate can reach epic proportions, along with relentless ruthlessness. Yes, it's sad what evil can be perpetrated by man left to himself without a Savior. In that time, having your hooves torn off might not be considered that big a deal.

It really does amaze me that people can think and say to themselves that humans are basically "good" – when the volumes of evidence we see going on around us is to the contrary. We have nothing good within us, and we have no capacity to generate any good either. Check out **Isaiah 64:6**, as well as **Romans 3:10** if you don't believe me. That's why I can't understand how we can refuse the love, mercy, and compassion shown by our Father in heaven through His Son. But we need to know this, we are refusing the One Who seeks us, and longs to bring us into His fold . . .

Matthew 9:35-36 – And Jesus was going about all the cities and the villages, teaching in their synagogues, and proclaiming the gospel of the kingdom, and healing every kind of disease and every kind of sickness. ³⁶ And seeing the multitudes, He felt compassion for them, because they were distressed and downcast like sheep without a shepherd.

We are the sheep and Jesus Christ is the Shepherd. We are the lost, the helpless to help ourselves, and the harassed. Christ alone is the One true Shepherd and He alone can save us from all of our sorrows. Jesus has saved us by His sacrifice and shed blood on the Cross. He paid the price that we can't even begin to think about paying. We, each and every one of us, are bought with the biggest price-tag in all of the Cosmos and all of eternity! All of our efforts at payment for our own sins are as "filthy rags" and not worthy of the love Christ demonstrates to us and the rest of the world. What do we do with this wonderful gift He persistently offers us? We don't even give Him ten or fifteen minutes of our day in prayer and the reading of His Word, because we are too busy and too wrapped up in ourselves. All the while, we moan and groan about our plight . . . and guess what – He listens to us and loves us anyway. Yes He's there, yes He's ready to help us, and yes, He's seeking us to the ends of the earth. And yes, He and the Holy Spirit pray for us constantly as it says in **Romans 8**. Part of the problem is, we are not looking for Him. And you and I know people out there who would ask Him to not even bother praying for them anyway.

Have you been healed by the wounds of Jesus Christ? If you haven't, please do so now . . . before all heck breaks loose and you are realizing you've missed the grace and mercy that He and He alone has provided for you. If you do, part of the byproduct may be that your marriage and family sees the grace and mercy of Jesus Christ spill over into your relationships with them. How life-changing would that be?

1 Peter 2:24-25 – and He Himself bore our sins in His body on the cross, that we might die to sin and live to righteousness; for by His wounds you were healed. ²⁵ For you were continually straying like sheep, but now you have returned to the Shepherd and Guardian of your souls.

A lot of us would say we've returned to our Savior. Speaking is a lot easier than doing wouldn't you say? Let me share with you something I've learned since I wrote my first book. Most people in our society today don't read. "Oh, I'm dyslexic . . ." is a common excuse. Or, "I can't focus long enough to read anything." Or, "I'm ADD." Or the most common excuse of all, "I'm just too busy to read anything, Mark."

There are more than 4000 copies of my first book out . . . most of them given away by yours truly. Since it has been out for about four years, most of those I've given it to have had some time to read it, but the vast majority haven't. "Aha!" you say, "That's to be expected when you've written a cruddy book!" I would say, "Touché! Point well-taken!" The problem with that is – I've had some people read that book two, three, and four times, and then call me to tell me how much it has impacted them. These people also say that they've enjoyed its content more each time they've read it. Others have asked me when I'm writing another book; that the first one left them wanting more. Some have told me that they are using it as a daily devotional book. I've had some people come back and buy as many as 60 copies to give out to their family and friends, after I had given them the first one. And No! – These are not family members who have done this. On multiple occasions, I've had people come up to me and say, "Why didn't you tell me that this thing got so good in the last half? I'd have finished it a lot sooner." But by far, the most common response I receive by those who have actually read and finished the book is this, "I'm going to read it again, there is so much in it."

Let me tell you about Cindy, a gal who read my first book . . .

Cindy had the copy of my book I had given her for about six months. She is a friend and a patient and was in my office visiting with me about her business. I don't know why, but I asked her if she had read my book. Sheepishly, she looked at me and said, "No Mark, I haven't read it. I'm just too busy!"

I then leaned forward and looked her in the eye and said with a little forcefulness, "Cindy . . . READ THAT BOOK!"

She looked a little puzzled and said, "Okay, I'll do it."

It was two weeks later on a Monday morning when I noticed a sticky-note placed on my desk. It said, "Cindy called and wants you to call her ASAP!" I thought she might have a toothache, so I called her right away. She said, "Mark, I read your book in two days this past weekend. Have you got twenty more copies that I can buy? I'm going home to Oklahoma this weekend and my entire family needs to read this book! I'm worried about where they are going to spend eternity!"

For the past seven months since, Cindy has started attending BSF – Bible Study Fellowship, and she's bought sixty books from me, and has had me order thirteen Bibles for her to give out to family and friends. What happened? It wasn't my book . . . it was the Holy Spirit that convicted her, changed her, and opened her eyes to the eternal perspective as opposed to the worldly perspective she had been focused on. She is on fire for Christ and impacting those in her family, as well as those who the Lord brings across her path.

Why do I belabor and point to the fact that I have to almost twist arms to get people to read? It's because it is true. I'm telling you, most people don't read! Reading takes time and reading takes effort and when you get down to the brass tacks, people don't make the time, and they don't make the effort to read . . . period. Our kids and even most adults get all their information off of the TV or from videos on the internet. Oh sure, they'll read adds about sales for stuff, or read about entertainers, or read about sports, or short articles on fashion or fishing. But to make time to read from God's Holy Word . . . forget about it! People don't want to look at it. Do you know why? It reminds them that they are fallen and that they are sinners. And we don't like to think of ourselves in those terms. We'd rather lie to ourselves and think that everything is A-Okay and that we are really pretty good people. If you ever do start the habit of reading . . . get ready – there's a whole new world out there for you to explore! Just be sure and pick meaningful books to read – like the ones in the Bibliography at the end of this book.

Like I've said, lip service is easy; reading takes time and effort. God speaks to "lip service" in His Word. Check it out . . .

Isaiah 29:11-14 – And the entire vision shall be to you like the words of a sealed book, which when they give it to the one who is literate, saying, "Please read this," he will say, "I cannot, for it is sealed." 12 Then the book will be given to the one who is illiterate, saying, "Please read this." And he will say, "I cannot read." 13 Then the Lord said, "Because this people draw near with their words And honor Me with their lip service, But they remove their hearts far from Me, And their reverence for Me consists of tradition learned *by rote*, [14] Therefore behold, I will once again deal marvelously with this people, wondrously marvelous; And the wisdom of their wise men shall perish, And the discernment of their discerning men shall be concealed."

So you might say, "So what if the wise men perish? It's no big deal." You really might want to reconsider that statement. Look at what the Lord says in the next two verses . . .

Isaiah 29:15-16 – Woe to those who deeply hide their plans from the LORD, And whose deeds are *done* in a dark place, And they say, "Who sees us?" or "Who knows us?" [16] You turn *things* around! Shall the potter be considered as equal with the clay, That what is made should say to its maker, "He did not make me"; Or what is formed say to him who formed it, "He has no understanding "?

Do you really think you can turn the tables on the God of the universe? Do you think you're going to shake your fist at Him and make Him quiver? Don't think for one nanosecond that you can escape God's courtroom. We will each be on trial one day and God will be the Judge. Satan will be the Accuser, and Jesus Christ will be the Advocate. Unless of course you don't want an Advocate to represent you. You may say, "I'll just represent myself, I've been more good than bad." If that is the case, get ready. You are in for a huge wake-up call! You might want to leave that defense at home, and rely on the only Advocate Who can save you, because your defense will absolutely not cut it . . .

1 John 2:1-2 – My little children, I am writing these things to you that you may not sin. And if anyone sins, we have an Advocate with the Father, Jesus Christ the righteous; ² and He Himself is the propitiation for our sins; and not for ours only, but also for *those of* the whole world.

James 2:10 – For whoever keeps the whole law and yet stumbles in one *point*, he has become guilty of all.

We know that we have all sinned many times, not just once. Since we know that we are sinners, we need an Advocate. That Advocate is Jesus Christ and Him alone. He is the propitiation or "atoning sacrifice" for our sins. No one else is the perfect sacrifice for us. No one else can even think about approaching Christ's perfection. He alone offers to save us with His atoning blood and pay the price we can't possibly pay. So you say, "Okay . . . I'll bite! I'll receive Jesus Christ as my Lord and Savior . . . and only hope. What now?"

Seek Him, earnestly seek Him. Give Christ the time and relationship He deserves . . . and we don't. Take that step that will help save your soul, save your marriage, save your kids, and possibly save all of them for eternity. Draw near to God and He will draw near to you . . .

James 4:8 – Draw near to God and He will draw near to you. Cleanse your hands, you sinners; and purify your hearts, you double-minded.

If you do take that first step toward Christ, He will enable you to avail yourself to Him more and more; drawing you closer and closer to Himself. Then you will find that you are wanting to learn more and more about the true Savior Who redeems you from sin, death, and yourself. You will probably find that you are a better reader than you thought. Only now you will WANT to make the time and you will WANT to make the effort to get to know Christ on a more intimate level.

> Joshua 1:7-9 – "Only be strong and very courageous; be careful to do according to all the law which Moses My servant commanded you; do not turn from it to the right or to the left, so that you may have success wherever you go. 8 "This book of the law shall not depart from your mouth, but you shall meditate on it day and night, so that you may be careful to do according to all that is written in it; for then you will make your way prosperous, and then you will have success. 9 "Have I not commanded you? Be strong and courageous! Do not tremble or be dismayed, for the LORD your God is with you wherever you go."

When you take that step, you may find your spouse and or your family, looking at you a little funny. That's okay! Christ, through the Holy Spirit is starting to change you and doing so for the better. You may find you are not quite "on edge" as much as you used to be. You may even find yourself letting stuff slide that you wouldn't have let slide before. That's okay too! Again, you are changing from being self-centered to being centered on God and others. You may even like that person looking back at you in the mirror each morning a little better. Yes, you might even look forward to getting up earlier in the morning, just so you can spend more time praying and reading God's Word. When you do, get ready because your whole world is about to change. The "lip-service" starts to be getting left behind as you start showing the love of Christ . . .

James 1:25 – But one who looks intently at the perfect law, the *law* of liberty, and abides by it, not having become a forgetful hearer but an effectual doer, this man shall be blessed in what he does.

Being a person of the Word doesn't mean you won't sin . . . you will. It doesn't mean you'll be perfect . . . you won't be. It doesn't mean you'll be the perfect spouse or parent . . . you'll still make mistakes. But one thing will be sure, when you are seeking Christ earnestly, Satan will not take you captive for the long-haul of eternity. Quite the contrary, you'll find rest from the angst, fear, "AND" trepidation this world tries to heap upon you. Because you now "know the program" – and the program means you'll be in heaven for eternity with Jesus Christ and His followers!

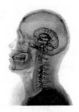

CHAPTER 7 – I

It's all about "ME!" Have you heard of the "Me Generation"? I don't know why one particular generation has been given that name, because frankly, it could and should be the name of every generation. We, as sinners, are obsessed with ourselves, and have been so from the very beginning. It doesn't take long to visit with someone and get a pretty good idea as to what motivates them. Most of the time it's their money, power, recognition, or possessions. Whatever makes them look good and have others looking at them and their stuff with covetous eyes is a real turn on. We like being the center of attention don't we? And yet this is another nail in the coffin of marriage and family unity. So long to the Lord's call to serve others, much less our spouse or kids. Sure, family may get served as a by-product of all of our efforts, but who we are most concerned about really serving is ourselves.

We have lapsed into what I call an "I Coma" in our country today and it looks like we don't have much chance of coming out of it. Even when we do go and serve others, it is usually for self-recognition and with hidden selfish motives. Not so? I don't see too many Mother Teresa's walking around out there, do you?

This happens all the time to me. Someone says, "Hey Doc,

I've got someone from my church that really needs some help with their teeth . . . can you help them?" I tell them to send them in and I'll take a look at them for no charge. Nine times out of ten, the poor person has a huge mess that has either come from a phobia of dentistry or a long history of neglect. When I tell their friend who sent them in that I'll be happy to help them and pitch-in – along with them, to take care of the person's needs, the interest and empathy for the person seems to fade really fast. In other words, they want things for those they want to help out . . . they just don't want to participate by having to put any "skin in the game." Oh, they'll make the contact for them, but when it comes to helping to pay the price . . . forget it; money's too hard to come by.

I must confess, in many ways, I'm just as guilty as anybody of being in my self-serving "I Coma". How many times have "I" lost "my" blessing in heaven by telling people of the things "I've" done for others through "my" walk of faith, teaching "my" Sunday School class, or the first book "I" published. I need to get out of my own "I Coma". It's similar to how I share with people that Keyea tells me that I am a "Legend in my own mind!" . . . when she has never actually told me that. Call it what it really is – it's false humility. One of my mentors told me one time, "You know Mark – Humility is an elusive thing . . . once you think you've got it – it's gone!"

We show similar traits in the way we treat those in our family. We want them there when we need them, just don't ask us to sacrifice any of our favorite activities to work on our relationship with them when it's inconvenient for us. After all, I work hard, and it's my happiness and contentment that counts. They are responsible for their own needs. Or as some might say, "You know, my wife really doesn't get it, she needs to pony-up and quit whining about everything she's unhappy with. She's got it better than most wives."

This just doesn't fit with what God tells us in His instruction book . . .

Ephesians 5:25 – Husbands, love your wives, just as Christ also loved the church and gave Himself up for her;

Guys, we just want to focus on our wives doing the "submissive" thing, not on us doing the "loving" and "giving-up" thing. This is where I do have to chalk one up for the ladies. I don't know if you're married or not, but one thing I can tell you about my house is this; there's "magic" going on all the time! You don't believe me do you? It's true . . . way true! Listen, when I go to open up my sock drawer to get some clean socks – they're there. It's magic! When I go to the fridge to get some milk for my coffee – it's there. It's magic! When I get in that shower stall – it's clean and not cruddy. It's magic! Get the picture? My wife works really hard to keep everything in the house taken care of for our family.

Yes, I know guys, you can turn that "magic" thing around and say, "But I make the money so she can buy the socks and milk and cleaning supplies." This is true as well, but we as the spiritual leaders of our families, need to get out of our "I Coma"! If we don't, there's going to be hell to pay . . .

Zephaniah 1:12-18 – "And it will come about at that time That I will search Jerusalem with lamps, And I will punish the men Who are stagnant in spirit, Who say in their hearts, 'The LORD will not do good or evil!' [13] "Moreover, their wealth will become plunder, And their houses desolate; Yes, they will build houses but not inhabit *them*, And plant vineyards but not drink their wine." [14] Near is the great day of the LORD,

Near and coming very quickly; Listen, the day of the LORD! In it the warrior cries out bitterly. [15] A day of wrath is that day, A day of trouble and distress, A day of destruction and desolation, A day of darkness and gloom, A day of clouds and thick darkness, [16] A day of trumpet and battle cry, Against the fortified cities And the high corner towers. [17] And I will bring distress on men, So that they will walk like the blind, Because they have sinned against the LORD; And their blood will be poured out like dust, And their flesh like dung. [18] Neither their silver nor their gold Will be able to deliver them On the day of the LORD's wrath; And all the earth will be devoured In the fire of His jealousy, For He will make a complete end, Indeed a terrifying one, Of all the inhabitants of the earth.

We don't want to be "stagnant in spirit" do we? That is just what we become when we get so into ourselves and lose sight of what is really important. This description of these days sounds like a very dismal time. This time is brought about because of the sins of mankind against God. Would you say that we, as a nation, with our misguided values and priorities, are on this path to destruction? Many would say that we definitely are on this path, and the marriages and families that are strewn by the wayside are further evidence that this is so.

So what do we do? What can we do in the onslaught of this destruction? We can do what we should have been doing all along. We can do what our Lord tells us to do in His Word. Instead of focusing on ourselves and our needs we can become the servant we should be for our Savior. We can lose our lives for Christ's sake, and for the sake of those around us.

Matthew 16:24-25 – Then Jesus said to His disciples, "If anyone wishes to come after Me, let him deny himself, and take up his cross, and follow Me. ²⁵ "For whoever wishes to save his life shall lose it; but whoever loses his life for My sake shall find it.

After thirty-one years in prayer and Bible study, being on a reading frenzy of books by giants of the faith, and teaching Sunday School classes for some thirty years; I've learned something. You have to understand; I'm pretty thick-skulled and it takes me a while to learn things, but the Lord finally got the message across and has helped reveal something to me that has impacted my walk of faith greatly. The revelation He has given me is that I have to . . . "Die to self!" Yes, I have to say "good-bye" to the old me, myself, and I. The other revelation He has shown me is that this "Die to self" quest is difficult. I have been praying the following prayer for myself for the last couple of years, and I still find myself wanting to usurp control all the time. However, through the indwelling Holy Spirit, the Lord is helping me to make inroads in this endeavor. Here's the prayer I've been praying . . .

"Dear Father in heaven, You know that I come to You on my knees and with all the worship, reverence, and submission I can . . . and I thank You for the gift of my salvation through the shed blood of my Lord and Savior Jesus Christ, Your Son. I am a lowly sinner and there is nothing good within me whatsoever! I have no righteousness of my own . . . only the righteousness You clothe me with through Your Son. Please forgive me of my many sins . . . those that I commit against You each and every day.

I ask You Father, please help me to die to myself . . . empty me of myself, and You fill me with your Holy Spirit . . . fill me full of You throughout this day. Give me Your eyes Lord Jesus, that I might see the opportunities You bring to me. Empower me and give me Your mind Lord Jesus, that I might more and more have the mind of Christ . . . which will enable me to show Your love Lord Jesus to those that You send my way. In Your holy and precious name I pray Lord Jesus. Amen."

Romans 5:1-6 – Therefore having been justified by faith, we have peace with God through our Lord Jesus Christ, ² through whom also we have obtained our introduction by faith into this grace in which we stand; and we exult in hope of the glory of God. ³ And not only this, but we also exult in our tribulations, knowing that tribulation brings about perseverance; ⁴ and perseverance, proven character; and proven character, hope; ⁵ and hope does not disappoint, because the love of God has been poured out within our hearts through the Holy Spirit who was given to us. ⁶ For while we were still helpless, at the right time Christ died for the ungodly.

Like I say, I've seen Him making slight inroads in transforming me more and more into His likeness . . . that of being a servant . . . as Paul tells us in **Philippians 2**. He has shown me evidence in my life and actions that allow me to see that He is answering my prayer. The old self with its wrongful desires is dying and being mortified. The new and regenerated self is being built-up and manifested – granted, some days more than others . . . but still there all the same. Old ways and old selves die hard, and it takes time for the Lord to enable them to do so.

Ephesians 4:20-24 – But you did not learn Christ in this way, ²¹ if indeed you have heard Him and have

been taught in Him, just as truth is in Jesus, [22] that, in reference to your former manner of life, you lay aside the old self, which is being corrupted in accordance with the lusts of deceit, [23] and that you be renewed in the spirit of your mind, [24] and put on the new self, which in *the likeness of* God has been created in righteousness and holiness of the truth.

So with Christ, through the indwelling Holy Spirit becoming greater, and the old me becoming lesser, I am finding that there is a boldness that seems to be taking over me more and more. That boldness is that I know Jesus Christ is my Savior and I don't have reservations of what others think of my faith in Christ anymore. I want others to know I'm a Christian and I want people to ask me questions about my Savior. I don't want to be a sledge-hammer, beating others up for my Lord. I want to show them His love and be a stepping-stone for them to be drawn to Christ and Him alone. I want them to have this same blessed happiness that He has formed within me. I am not ashamed of Jesus Christ any longer . . .

Romans 1:16 – For I am not ashamed of the gospel, for it is the power of God for salvation to everyone who believes, to the Jew first and also to the Greek.

Not being ashamed of Him allows me to come out of the "I Coma" and kill the "I" of self-centeredness. Losing the "I" then enables me to submit to the real and great "I AM!" . . . the One I should be submitted to anyway. And doing that leads to the greatest freedom in the world. That freedom comes because I can submit to His wondrous plan while letting go of my own puny plans. This is when the real happiness starts. The real love and zeal for life is made manifest to those around my sphere of influence. I don't have to worry about my plan, because I know that His plan is better than anything I can envision or come up with. All I have to do is to follow Him daily . . .

> **Jeremiah 29:11-13 – 'For I know the plans that I have for you,' declares the LORD, 'plans for welfare and not for calamity to give you a future and a hope. [12] "Then you will call upon Me and come and pray to Me, and I will listen to you. [13] 'And you will seek Me and find *Me*, when you search for Me with all your heart.**

The one thing I do know that I need to help me stay focused on His plan, and His will while not being diverted off path to my own, is that I have to stay in prayer to Him, as well as in His Word – on a daily basis. God can change me more and more into the likeness of His Son Jesus Christ, if and only if, I stay in communion with Him. This helps keep my focus on Christ and off of my own wishes, but it doesn't take long to lose this focus if I'm not careful. In just a few days off from spending time with Him, I can see and feel tangible evidence that I'm growing further and further away from my Savior. When I have taken time off from being in His Word and in prayer, I find the separation is significant and substantial. Then getting back into His mindset and will is more and more difficult, the longer I stay away from Him. Keep in mind, God hasn't moved away from me, I'm the one who's moved away from Him.

This point is well illustrated in comments I received from a very close friend who had wandered from his faith in Christ. He had not turned his back on Jesus, he'd just gotten lost in pursuing other things that garnered his attention at a particular time in his life about 10 years ago.

Here is what he shared with me after reading the manuscript for this book . . .

"Mark – The book is a reflection of all you have mentored me on over the past twenty years. It took medical issues in my life for God to get my attention because most of the time, for various reasons, I did not want to listen. The change in my life occurred once I began the discipline of reading the Bible EVERY morning and praying. Then I wanted to be back in church . . . then I wanted to be involved in ministry.

Slowly I am being transformed into the family spiritual leader I should have always been. God has helped me to reduce my self-centeredness, and focus more on Him, and those around me. I felt the book tracks many of the thought processes as the Holy Spirit indwells us and then transforms our lives to be more Christ-like. No doubt it is a life-long process, but for me, there is peace in knowing I am on the right track and I am seeing my life being of better use for my Savior."

This is what I'm talking about – staying in communion and relationship with Jesus Christ our Savior on a daily basis in His Word and in prayer, then enables us to get our focus off of ourselves and onto Him and those He sends our way. The Holy Spirit is filling us more and more through our earnestly seeking Christ, and gives us wisdom, discernment, understanding, and insight – so that we have the "mind" and "eyes" of Christ, thus being able to show those around us the "love" of Christ! And we do it all for His glory!

So, hear me out. If we stay in God's Word each day . . . And if we commune with God in prayer each and every day . . . And if He enables us to die to ourselves and get out of our "I Coma" . . . and if He allows us to be emptied of ourselves and filled with His Holy Spirit . . .

It is then, yes then . . . that we will be able, through the Holy

Spirit indwelling in us . . . to say to our God and our Savior . . . "Here am I. Send me!"

Isaiah 6:8 – Then I heard the voice of the Lord, saying, "Whom shall I send, and who will go for Us?" Then I said, "Here am I. Send me!"

And God will send us. He will send us right to where He needs and wants us. And there, we will see opportunities galore . . . that He has put us right in the midst of, in order that we might serve Him, by serving those He brings to us. In doing this, we will start to see fruit – bountiful fruit – being born for God and His kingdom. And seeing this harvest, that is all of Christ and not by our own efforts, He will be using us as we avail ourselves to Him. This is the truly happy and fulfilled life. The life of eternal and lasting happiness to have been so blessed that Christ has enabled us to be a lasting part of His plan for eternity . . . in drawing others to Himself, for His glory. These others who are drawn to faith in Christ may be our spouse, our kids, our parents, siblings, distant relatives, friends, co-workers, or strangers.

Isn't it amazing? That the God and King of the universe can use knucklehead sinners like us, to help Him further His kingdom – what a miracle!

John 6:38 – "For I have come down from heaven, not to do My own will, but the will of Him who sent Me.

Thus, we end up doing the will of God the Father and not our own. We end up serving our family's needs, as well as the needs of others around us, because we are finally doing the will of the One Who sent us. It is the reason that I am here . . . which I stated at the end of the first book . . ." I am here to serve the Lord Who sent me; to serve those He sends to me; with reverence and humility . . . for His glory."

I can honestly say that I have no claim now . . . and never have had a claim on me finding my Savior. I would have never chose Christ and didn't want to. Looking back over the life I've lived, I know that I was absolutely drawn to Jesus Christ by God the Father. If it hadn't been for Him pursuing me, I wouldn't have ever been drawn to Christ . . .

John 6:44 – "No one can come to Me, unless the Father who sent Me draws him; and I will raise him up on the last day.

One of the things the Lord will help us to do in order to serve Him and our family's best interest is to "die to self!" – but we have to be willing to do so. We have to be willing to get out of our "I Coma" . . . and Jesus Christ has provided the only way for that to happen!

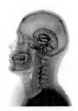

CHAPTER 8 – MARRIED

Hebrews 13:4 – *Let* **marriage** *be held* **in honor among all, . . .**

The definition of marriage in our society and culture seems to be changing. It's perplexing and frustrating to most of us that Judges on the bench can arbitrarily and on a whim go against the overwhelming beliefs of the majority of the people in this country. Time after time the people have voted their conscience and stated unequivocally that marriage is between one man and one woman. Heck, even Phil Robertson caused a ruckus when he made the same statement by reading a verse out of the Bible regarding marriage. He received tremendous support for his stance from the majority of down-home Americans, but the mainstream media excoriated him . . . as they do anyone who makes a stance for God and His Holy Word. State that you believe God's Word, and that the Bible is God's true Word with no errors and no missteps, and you are labeled an imbecile and a moron by the elitist upper echelon of the left in our country. Most of these just can't let their pride and ego go. They can't give credit to anyone other than themselves for anything good, and that nothing good in our country comes from the Holy and One True God of the universe. They shake their fist at Him and tout their unbelief in the Savior, but one day they will bow their knees and with their lips declare that He and He alone is God almighty. Just go to **Philippians 2** and take a look at that chapter.

The design for marriage should follow God's definition; not mankind's.

God has a perfect design for marriage and He alludes to it in Genesis . . .

Genesis 2:24 – For this cause a man shall leave his father and his mother, and shall cleave to his wife; and they shall become one flesh.

Keyea and I are a dying breed! Yes, we are getting older and I'm looking the part, even if my lovely wife isn't. You see, we come from homes where our parents "stayed the course" in their marriages. My parents were married some fifty-two years when my Mother died of cancer. Keyea's parents were one month shy of being married for sixty years when her Dad passed. You don't hear of many couples that have those kinds of examples to grow up and observe from, especially both the husband and wife, as in our marriage. This type of situation is really getting to be the exception, rather than the rule; which it used to be. The marriages of our parents showed us too many things to count and describe to you, but bear with me as I try to share a few things I observed from them.

One thing was that their marriages were not perfect. There were things, even after fifty and sixty years that got on their nerves about each other. They still had their differences of opinions and their differences of likes and dislikes. Which means there were times they were upset with one another. I don't mean knock-down, drag-out fights, but times that they were at-odds with one another to a degree that was observable, both to family and friends. I never heard loud and boisterous arguments or overly heated words from either couple, but there were times they did seem to have a "low-burn" going on because they were upset. That helped me to see from them a commitment that is uncommon now days. They were committed to one another, to their families, and to their marriage.

Another observation was that they seemingly kept their differences and disagreements to themselves. They kept their issues or dislikes private. Of course there was no Facebook, Twitter, or internet with which to communicate their variances to the world as there is today. I think this is a significant problem that we deal with that our previous generation didn't have to worry about. They couldn't "post" those problematic statements and photos that would be out there in cyberspace for the long haul. They couldn't do a Google search to find an old high school flame to try to rekindle their old high school love life when their marriage had flickered-out! Their lives weren't as in-touch with so many relationships that required attention. Their attention was on their marriage and their kids, not on what all their acquaintances' families were doing. Oh sure, the gossip was still common, but by and large, before the internet and reality shows, our parents didn't have the incessant bombardment of myriads of poor examples of the modern family which goes on today.

They also considered that they had equal ownership of their possessions. I don't remember his and hers checking accounts. What THEY had was THEIRS, not yours or mine. Our parents didn't count on divorce they counted on staying together and making their marriage work for the long term.

Along with the one checking account and nest egg, they were careful to live within their means. They did so without living out a destitute and deprived lifestyle. They had fun and enjoyed playing bridge and dominos with other couples, while the kids were outside playing tag or climbing trees. We would take family vacations with close family friends and hang out at the lake waterskiing.

This is a similar lifestyle that Keyea and I have followed with our family as well. We have close friends that we go snow-skiing with each year, and we've enjoyed watching our kids grow up together with their daughter. The three of our kids have a special bond that transcends them having to get together often as all our lives are so busy. But when they do get to hang-out together it is right back to the "old days" of their laughing and screaming as they zig-zag down through the trees on the ski runs. Just last week, my daughter reminded me of the old-days.

Kailey, is an architecture major and graduating from Texas A&M this year. For some reason, she and our son Joseph seem subtly drawn to 1970's culture. Joseph loves the music and cars from back then, and Kailey loves the architecture and music as well. Yesterday she sent her Mom and me an email with photos of a vintage 70's style house with the interior decorating to match. It helped me to ponder again the families of friends I had while in my high school years because it looked so familiar to the houses of my friends back then. I had very few friends whose parents were divorced, and I felt like part of the families of all my friends. If you wanted to see pictures of your friends, you either looked through a photo album, or sat down for a long slide show projected on the family room wall. The only instant photo was a Polaroid that you had to pull from the back of a camera and wipe with a sticky material to try to help preserve it.

While the 70's family wasn't perfection personified, there was a lot less busyness, a lot less birth out of wedlock, a lot fewer kids growing up in single-parent homes, and no internet. There weren't as many blended families, nor nearly as many kids growing up without a Dad in the home. There was no sharing of photos of kids in the nude on their phones with one another, and no text related bullying or suicides. The divorce rate was significant, but not of the rampant nature we see today. Also, there was seemingly far less frequency of kids having kids. I mean, think about it . . . day-care centers in High Schools . . . seriously? All this to say that it sure is obvious that everything is really kicking into overdrive when it comes to the decisions we have to make, and there is no going back to the good ole' days.

It is obvious we are living in much different times and a much different society and culture than was present even twenty or thirty years ago. Warp-speed is the pace, and downward spiral is the direction we are headed in. While we can't get back to the good ole' days, we can stop and pause to see what is pressing in on our families. Like the out of control decision-making we find ourselves in most of the time we stop and look around. It's those blasted "tyrannies" coming into our lives. The "tyrannies" of the urgent, possessions, meaningless conversations, self-centeredness, and what others will think. The parents over work & have too many things to look after. The kids have too many sports activities, as well as after-school events. All these "things" put undue stress on both individuals, and families. There is no way we can even think about having the time to become "one flesh" with our spouse.

"One flesh" . . . now that's a concept . . . To even approach this as a couple is almost nonexistent these days. The truth is we are so into me, myself, and I that we can't even conceive of this as a possibility, let alone something doable. So we end up with marriages that are hanging by a thread.

Another thing I noticed with both her Mom and my Dad after their spouses passed was this: the spouse left behind looked like they had each had half their heart ripped out of their chest, and it didn't stop. They truly had been together so long and grown so very close, that they were "one flesh!" You see, they had experienced what marriage is supposed to be; the melding of two people into one. This is what our God intended for us in our marriages, but it is vanishing right before our eyes at break-neck speed! So how can we, in our marriages today, achieve this "one flesh" completion?

Hebrews 13:4 – *Let* **marriage** *be held* **in honor among all,**

A pivotal thing that we must do is to honor the marriage vows we make to one another and to our God. We must take seriously our commitment to God, one another, and our families and stay the course for better or for worse, in sickness and in health . . . till death do us part. That stick-to-itiveness will result in another needed aspect in attaining the "one flesh" result we and our God desire.

I have to interject this story here because it's way too perfect an example to pass up . . .

There were rose pedals strewn on top of the intimate table for two on the back wall of the very nice restaurant. Yes, it was a nicely added touch to the special evening dinner celebration of Keyea and my 30th wedding anniversary. I had done myself proud and was thankful that all the plans were coming together so perfectly . . .

Before the first course was served, I thought the timing was exquisite for me to let Keyea know just how much she has meant to me through all these years. So I said to her, "Keyea, you are the love of my life . . . the best friend I have . . . the soul-mate that the Lord meant for me to have . . . in fact, you're a saint! Thank you for staying with me and sticking it out for all these years, Sweetie! I love you!"

Keyea gazed back at me with her beautiful eyes and replied, "Mark, you don't understand . . . the ONLY reason that I'm still with you is that I fear CHANGE . . . AND was worried that the next guy I got would be even worse than you!"

Ahhhhh! The bliss of love that envelopes us at these times is stunning, right? We both busted out laughing and you just have to understand that this is my wife and I love her so much I could bust!

Again, marriage takes commitment and there have been times in our marriage where it could have gone either way. I thank my Lord and Savior – and my wife – that she has stayed the course with me.

Staying the course will give our marriages the much-needed component of time together. This is huge, and is one of the biggest road blocks to us growing together into one flesh. We don't give our marriages time.

You may be thinking at this point, "But Mark, I've given this marriage way too much time already . . . this guy is NOT gonna change!" I don't know your situation and I can't give you advice, because I'm not qualified. Only you, your spouse, and the Lord can make the proper decision on what the three of you know needs to be done with your marriage. Whether it includes marriage counseling as a couple, individually – with or without kids, the complexities of the families out there today are many. It is amazing that many families make it for any length of time at all, much less for the rest of their lives. One thing is seemingly very consistent. Those families who are centered on Jesus Christ have a better chance of survival. Notice that I didn't say, "Those families that go to church." In fact, the divorce rate seems to be in pretty close proximity between Christians and non-believers. Let me state a known fact, that all of us going to church know all too well. Merely going to church, even if it involves going to church every Sunday morning, Sunday night, and every night of the week, does not make one a true brother or sister in Christ.

This brings up the other component that we must have in order to achieve the oneness our Lord and Savior wants for our marriages. It involves each of our individual relationship with Jesus Christ. The possibility of having a strong marriage is virtually nil without both spouses having a true and loving relationship with Jesus Christ. We may have our marriages, and we may have a lot of time under our belts with our marriage – but if we don't have Jesus Christ at the forefront of our marriage, we are fighting a very uphill battle to have our marriage, and our family be what it is supposed to be. Take a look at the diagram on the next page and see if you find it helpful in looking at how our marriages can be strengthened through Christ.Needless to say, if one of the spouses decides he or she is not going to receive Christ as their Savior, the entire marriage and family is in serious jeopardy.

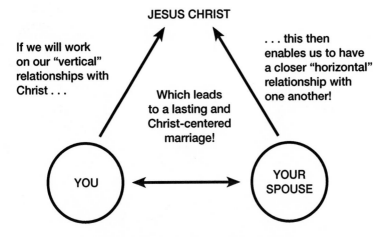

What leads to a successful marriage?

"MARRIAGE" in our present culture, society, and value system is at such a different place than it was thirty to forty years ago. And the way things are going, marriage is going to be perceived vastly different than it is now in the next few years. What is going on in our society today that has contributed to the "meltdown" of the marriage covenant? We have ourselves to blame, but there are so many places we could point to; such as our government, as well as our judicial system, and our amoral media. Then there's our individual self-centeredness, greed, envy, lust, and every other sin under the Sun. All these entities leave us repeatedly scratching our heads that we could be so far from where our God wants us to be in our family relationships. In the not-to-distant future, "MARRIAGE" will be even more unrecognizable and complex than it is now . . . believe me!

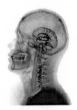

CHAPTER 9 – THEIR

What is "THEIR" opinion? Who are "THEY" – anyway? We always seem to be concerned as to what "THEIR" thoughts are on anything that we do. Most of the time it may be that we could say it is the world or the culture or society around us that we are trying to appease. Just where do they get their standards though? What is "THEIR" bottom line? What is "THEIR" rock bottom truth? I believe it is that there is no "absolute truth." There is no standard. There is no foundation of rock solid truth that the "THEIR" of the world stands on. That's how the "no absolute truth" majority of the world can dip, move, and jive to avoid being responsible for the decisions and maladies they place on those around them. It seems their mantra is: "Let's keep everything and everyone just off-center and off-balance enough to have no real cut and dry decisions that will cripple us if things don't work out the way we want them. If we are caught in lies and misdeeds, let's just move to a different topic that we can stir up enough controversy in to get people to forget the last controversy we started." Some would scoff at this notion and continue to put their heads in the sand. All the while it is being played out right in front of them, and they can't even see it.

Hence the "moving target" strategy plays right into the "no absolute truth" game plan that we find ourselves in. If you couple this with a compliant media that wants to play along at the "no absolute truth" game, then voila – the position and the topic of conversation is never given the opportunity to allow the public to stay on task long enough to have a meaningful dialogue on the many and diverse topics in order to impact productive change for the better.

The progressives are masters at this game of cat and mouse and they are playing the citizens of this country like a proverbial fiddle. There will be ramifications to all these plates being spun up in the air though. One day there will be a terrible crash, and not only those being played as the fiddle but those playing the fiddle will be caught up in the mess that ensues. Yes, we will be at a place that NONE of us wanted to be . . . and the hole we find ourselves in will be so huge and so deep that we will be aghast at the predicament that we have created for ourselves.

> Isaiah 1:4-6 – Alas, sinful nation, People weighed down with iniquity, Offspring of evildoers, Sons who act corruptly! They have abandoned the LORD, They have despised the Holy One of Israel, They have turned away from Him. ⁵ Where will you be stricken again, As you continue in *your* rebellion? The whole head is sick, And the whole heart is faint. ⁶ From the sole of the foot even to the head There is nothing sound in it, *Only* bruises, welts, and raw wounds, Not pressed out or bandaged, Nor softened with oil.

Phil Robertson of Duck Dynasty found out what it was like to take a stand that was opposed to "THEIR" thinking and he didn't back down. He stood his ground as we are told to do in **Ephesians 6**. His stance was that he agreed with what God says about marriage in the Bible.

There is a movement amongst a small percentage of our society to use their God given right of free speech to have their agenda forced on the rest of the people of this country who don't really agree with them. When those in the majority speak out, they are labeled and chastised as intolerant and bigoted. It's an old trick really and is being used very effectively by this small group. Major inroads to their cause have been accomplished because of a sympathetic media which slams the opposition to bits and pieces when they are trying to give a rebuttal.

We had another Man who stood His ground and didn't give in to what the "THEIR" of His time thought He should do while He was on this earth. His name is Jesus Christ and He is the ultimate authority, who will have all these critics bowing on their knees to Him one day. They had the opportunity to recognize Him for who He is, but they chose not to do so. Jesus Christ came to save sinners and yes, He even paid the price for "THEIR" sins as well . . . if they would just have come to Him. Listen to what the Bible says about our risen Savior, and what He came to eventually accomplish for all the "THEIR'S" who would turn against Him . . .

Revelation 21:3-4 – And I heard a loud voice from the throne, saying, "Behold, the tabernacle of God is among men, and He shall dwell among them, and they shall be His people, and God Himself shall be among them, ⁴ and He shall wipe away every tear from their eyes; and there shall no longer be *any* death; there shall no longer be *any* mourning, or crying, or pain; the first things have passed away."

You see, "THEY" didn't want His free gift . . . not then and not now. We are in enemy territory while here on this blue orb. Satan has a strangle-hold on the majority of the people on this planet and he has no intention of letting go. He won't win . . . he can't win . . . but he can make this earth a miserable place to be as long as he is given the opportunity by the God of the universe.

Yes, there is a choice and the sides are being delineated more and more as time goes on. People are either in one camp or another and the disparity is bordering on lunacy as we watch the respective forces play their hands in this serious game we call life on this earth. Check out what our Lord says about us as players . . . and who is going where when it all shakes out . . .

Psalm 1:1-6 – How blessed is the man who does not walk in the counsel of the wicked, Nor stand in the path of sinners, Nor sit in the seat of scoffers! [2] But his delight is in the law of the LORD, And in His law he meditates day and night. [3] And he will be like a tree *firmly* planted by streams of water, Which yields its fruit in its season, And its leaf does not wither; And in whatever he does, he prospers. [4] The wicked are not so, But they are like chaff which the wind drives away. [5] Therefore the wicked will not stand in the judgment, Nor sinners in the assembly of the righteous. [6] For the LORD knows the way of the righteous, But the way of the wicked will perish.

Many will perish but some will be brought up out of the pit of destruction, and will stand upon the rock that the Lord provides. The proud and those who perpetrate falsehood will not like the outcome they find themselves coming to bear.

But those who know the Lord and magnify His name will be carried and delivered under the Lord's care.

Psalm 40:2-17 – He brought me up out of the pit of destruction, out of the miry clay; And He set my feet upon a rock making my footsteps firm. ³ And He put a new song in my mouth, a song of praise to our God; Many will see and fear, And will trust in the LORD. ⁴ How blessed is the man who has made the LORD his trust, And has not turned to the proud, nor to those who lapse into falsehood. ⁵ Many, O LORD my God, are the wonders which Thou hast done, And Thy thoughts toward us; There is none to compare with Thee; If I would declare and speak of them, They would be too numerous to count. ⁶ Sacrifice and meal offering Thou hast not desired; My ears Thou hast opened; Burnt offering and sin offering Thou hast not required. ⁷ Then I said, "Behold, I come; In the scroll of the book it is written of me; ⁸ I delight to do Thy will, O my God; Thy Law is within my heart." ⁹ I have proclaimed glad tidings of righteousness in the great congregation; Behold, I will not restrain my lips, O LORD, Thou knowest. ¹⁰ I have not hidden Thy righteousness within my heart; I have spoken of Thy faithfulness and Thy salvation; I have not concealed Thy lovingkindness and Thy truth from the great congregation. ¹¹ Thou, O LORD, wilt not withhold Thy compassion from me; Thy lovingkindness and Thy truth will continually preserve me. ¹² For evils beyond number have surrounded me; My iniquities have overtaken me, so that I am not able to see; They are more numerous than the hairs of my head; And my heart has failed me. ¹³ Be pleased, O LORD, to deliver me; Make haste, O LORD, to help me. [14] Let those be ashamed and humiliated together Who seek my life to destroy it; Let those be turned back and dishonored Who delight in my hurt. [15] Let those be appalled because of their shame Who say to me, "Aha, aha!" [16] Let all who seek Thee rejoice and be glad in Thee; Let those who love Thy salvation say continually, "The LORD be magnified!" [17] Since I am afflicted and needy, Let the Lord be mindful of me; Thou art my help and my deliverer; Do not delay, O my God.

Let's take a look at what some of "THEIR" modes of operations are. It's evident that these are going on in our society at this present time. And the inexplicable nature of out and out lies that are stated time and time again are played over and over to a public that seems to be saying, "Wait a minute . . . I don't think that's true." But there it is played on the airwaves in immense repetitions over and over by those in power, as well as those in the mainstream media who seem to be saying, "Yes it is true . . . because there is no real truth . . . don't you know that? You idiot!" The Scriptures tell us that Satan is the father of lies. And Satan won't stop trying to prevent the real truth of the Bible to be considered in any form or fashion – even though it is the absolute truth.

Hence Satan keeps up the pressure and he has an all too willing menagerie of accomplices that he can rely on to do his bidding. They are so wrapped up in his rhetoric and falsehoods that they think they are the ones who are really privileged to be in the inner sanctum of his diabolical sanctuary. You know what? They are in his inner sanctum, and it's leading straight to hell in a hand-basket. They just don't recognize it for what it is. Their greed and pride have taken them over the edge of reason and they have no hope of ever coming back from the other side of darkness that they are in. That is unless the Lord provides a way for them to have their eyes opened and to be brought back. They exploit those they are given charge over and like their leader, the father of lies, they stick to their mode of operations to deceive and destroy any and all that they have a temporary control over.

2 Peter 2:2-3 – And many will follow their sensuality, and because of them the way of the truth will be maligned; ³ and in *their* greed they will exploit you with false words; their judgment from long ago is not idle, and their destruction is not asleep.

However, they will be judged and will have to pay the price for the sins they commit. God the Father, God the Son, and God the Holy Spirit will not rest until their judgment is carried out and meted out against those who made their stand against them. No matter how much the opposition tries to distort and decimate His Holy Word, God's truth will stand in His certainty and His power for eternity. The words of those who make a stance against God and His Word will seal their own destruction and they will rue the day they let their pride in their own "no absolute truth" stance take its place in their lives.

2 Peter 3:15-16 – and regard the patience of our Lord *to be* salvation; just as also our beloved brother Paul, according to the wisdom given him, wrote to you, ¹⁶ as also in all *his* letters, speaking in them of these things, in which are some things hard to understand, which the untaught and unstable distort, as *they do* also the rest of the Scriptures, to their own destruction.

No matter that they mock Him and His Word . . . it will all be as idle chatter, when they are brought to the realization that they chose the wrong side to be on when it comes to "absolute" vs. "no absolute" truth. They had their time, they achieved their goals and now it is over; it is time to pay the piper. The problem is that they will pay such a dear and catastrophic and eternal price! There is no going back and regrouping as if to say, "Oh I'm sorry . . . I really didn't mean it to come out that way. I really didn't realize that there actually is a true God and that this Bible book really is God's Holy Word." How this plays out is not up to me and my opinion, but one thing I can have confidence will happen – it will play out in accordance with God's Holy Word and will not contradict anything stated in it.

2 Peter 3:3-7 – Know this first of all, that in the last days mockers will come with *their* mocking, following after their own lusts, ⁴ and saying, "Where is the promise of His coming? For *ever* since the fathers fell asleep, all continues just as it was from the beginning of creation." ⁵ For when they maintain this, it escapes their notice that by the word of God *the* heavens existed long ago and *the* earth was formed out of water and by water, ⁶ through which the world at that time was destroyed, being flooded with water. ⁷ But the present heavens and earth by His word are being reserved for fire, kept for the day of judgment and destruction of ungodly men.

Yes, their mocking will be incessant and loud, and the truth will escape their notice. But the day-of-judgment will come and it will come swiftly and as sure as the Sun will come up tomorrow. The ungodly will be judged and their destruction will be sure and to their surprise.

However, it won't be a surprise to those who are of the faith who are sure and steadfast in Jesus Christ. It's not that the believers relish the judgment and destruction of those who have rejected God. But they realize that God's just and righteous wrath must be exercised against those who rush headlong into the error of worshipping the father of lies rather than the one true God. They are the tares among the wheat, the false among the true. They may have been able to fool many of the believers while sitting alongside of them in churches and Sunday school classes, but the vetting process will be sure and no mistakes will be made. Either their names appear in the Lamb's book of Life or they don't . . . and there will be no getting around the fact that they never were true in their faith in Jesus Christ – ever! They will have a reservation in the "black darkness" which has been reserved for them forever . . .

> **Jude 1:10-19 – But these men revile the things which they do not understand; and the things which they know by instinct, like unreasoning animals, by these things they are destroyed. [11] Woe to them! For they have gone the way of Cain, and for pay they have rushed headlong into the error of Balaam, and perished in the rebellion of Korah. [12] These men are those who are hidden reefs in your love feasts when they feast with you without fear, caring for themselves; clouds without water, carried along by winds; autumn trees without fruit, doubly dead, uprooted; [13] wild waves of the sea, casting up their own shame like foam; wandering stars, for whom the black darkness has been reserved forever. [14] And about these also Enoch, *in the seventh generation* from Adam, prophesied, saying, "Behold, the Lord came with many thousands of His holy ones,**

^{15} to execute judgment upon all, and to convict all the ungodly of all their ungodly deeds which they have done in an ungodly way, and of all the harsh things which ungodly sinners have spoken against Him." ^{16} These are grumblers, finding fault, following after their *own* lusts; they speak arrogantly, flattering people for the sake of *gaining an* advantage. ^{17} But you, beloved, ought to remember the words that were spoken beforehand by the apostles of our Lord Jesus Christ, ^{18} that they were saying to you, "In the last time there shall be mockers, following after their own ungodly lusts." ^{19} These are the ones who cause divisions, worldly-minded, devoid of the Spirit.

The only light in the darkness they are in for eternity will be the fire and brimstone that burns, but does not consume them. It will be a terrible place, one that we would wish on no one . . . not even the worst of those among us.

Revelation 21:8 – "But for the cowardly and unbelieving and abominable and murderers and immoral persons and sorcerers and idolaters and all liars, their part *will be* in the lake that burns with fire and brimstone, which is the second death."

The book of Life will not lie and will not contain the names of all the people who lived on this earth. Some will be so very surprised that they were deceived and their anguish will be eternal. Their deeds they thought were good works will be as nothing and have no capacity to help them avoid their doom.

Revelation 20:10-15 – And the devil who deceived them was thrown into the lake of fire and brimstone, where the beast and the false prophet are also; and they will be tormented day and night forever and ever. [11] And I saw a great white throne and Him who sat upon it, from whose presence earth and heaven fled away, and no place was found for them. [12] And I saw the dead, the great and the small, standing before the throne, and books were opened; and another book was opened, which is *the book* of life; and the dead were judged from the things which were written in the books, according to their deeds. [13] And the sea gave up the dead which were in it, and death and Hades gave up the dead which were in them; and they were judged, every one *of them* according to their deeds. [14] And death and Hades were thrown into the lake of fire. This is the second death, the lake of fire. [15] And if anyone's name was not found written in the book of life, he was thrown into the lake of fire.

However for those that believe, it will be a different story. They will experience the love of God, as well as the mercy of our Lord Jesus Christ. And they will have eternal life in heaven with their Father – the God of the universe who will love and provide for them always. The ecstasy and bliss will be unimaginable and unfathomable. Can you imagine standing in the presence of God Almighty and actually feeling that you belong there with Him – forever!!!

Jude 1:20-25 – But you, beloved, building yourselves up on your most holy faith; praying in the Holy Spirit; [21] keep yourselves in the love of God, waiting anxiously for the mercy of our Lord Jesus Christ to eternal life. [22] And have mercy on some, who are doubting; [23] save others, snatching them out of the fire; and on some have mercy with fear, hating even the garment polluted by the flesh. ²⁴ Now to Him who is able to keep you from stumbling, and to make you stand in the presence of His glory blameless with great joy, ²⁵ to the only God our Savior, through Jesus Christ our Lord, *be* glory, majesty, dominion and authority, before all time and now and forever. Amen.

Folks, that's why we are here – to join in our Lord and Savior's redemptive work by witnessing to those around us of Him, and thus enabling some to be "snatched from the fire." That's what we do . . . we love those "THEIRS" all the time they are ranting and raving and disagreeing with us. The God of the universe is the God of the impossible as well as the God of second chances. Where would those of us who do believe in Jesus Christ be if He wasn't? We would be right there with all the other "THEIRS" . . . in line for eternity in hell, so we don't need to get puffed-up at all about our position. We need to help others to get to that saved and eternal place we already know we are headed to through Jesus Christ.

Romans 8:5-14 – For those who are according to the flesh set their minds on the things of the flesh, but those who are according to the Spirit, the things of the Spirit. ⁶ For the mind set on the flesh is death, but the mind set on the Spirit is life and peace, ⁷ because the mind set on the flesh is hostile toward God; for it does not subject itself to the law of God, for it is not even able *to do so*; ⁸ and those who are in the flesh cannot please God. ⁹ However, you are not in the flesh but in the Spirit, if indeed the Spirit of God dwells in you. But if anyone does not have the Spirit of Christ, he does not belong to Him. ¹⁰ And if Christ is in you, though the body is dead because of sin, yet the spirit is alive because of righteousness. [11] But if the Spirit of Him who raised Jesus from the dead dwells in you, He who raised Christ Jesus from the dead will also give life to your mortal bodies through His Spirit who indwells you. [12] So then, brethren, we are under obligation, not to the flesh, to live according to the flesh— [13] for if you are living according to the flesh, you must die; but if by the Spirit you are putting to death the deeds of the body, you will live. [14] For all who are being led by the Spirit of God, these are sons of God.

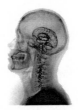

CHAPTER 10 – KING

Who and what is your "KING?" We each have a king that sits on the throne of our hearts, whether we want to admit it or not. Oh, the one who occupies the throne can and will change from time to time. But if we are honest with ourselves, most of us would readily admit that we each sit on that throne, and we are not giving up that position without a fight. Keep this in mind, Satan never gave up that position and look what it garnered him. One day there will be eternal separation between himself and God, and yes, he will get what he desires. God will be away from him and Satan won't have to be in God's presence anymore. The problem will be that he will be in the presence of God's wrath and judgment for eternity. And he will have no possible way to escape it. Satan and all those who want to be out of God's proximity will achieve their wishes and desires. I think when they get those wishes and realize there is no turning back, they will have the most unbelievable sense of regret, remorse, and sorrow at what they know could have been. They chose . . . and they chose wrong . . . and the king they decided to follow was not the true king.

Who is your king? Take a look at the King of all Kings that the Bible points us to . . .

Revelation 1:13-18 – and in the middle of the lampstands one like a son of man, clothed in a robe reaching to the feet, and girded across His breast with a golden girdle. [14] And His head and His hair were white like white wool, like snow; and His eyes were like a flame of fire; [15] and His feet _were_ like burnished bronze, when it has been caused to glow in a furnace, and His voice _was_ like the sound of many waters. [16] And in His right hand He held seven stars; and out of His mouth came a sharp two-edged sword; and His face was like the sun shining in its strength. [17] And when I saw Him, I fell at His feet as a dead man. And He laid His right hand upon me, saying, "Do not be afraid; I am the first and the last, [18] and the living One; and I was dead, and behold, I am alive forevermore, and I have the keys of death and of Hades.

We will all stand before this King, and we each will give an account of where He has stood in our lives on this earth. Knees will possibly be shaking, and heads will definitely be bowed. Some will be sobbing with tears of joy, while others will be shedding the other kind of tears . . . the ones we don't like to think about. They will be shedding tears over the realization of the lost state of their souls.

The saints on His right will be giddy with excitement. The fact that they put their faith in Jesus Christ will swell them up with the love of Christ and that He has given them His grace and mercy – enabling them to share in His inheritance for eternity. They probably won't even notice that there is another crowd across the way . . . and the mood is much different over there. The oppressive nature of anguish over what is coming next for them is their only focus, as they realize they've missed the opportunity for salvation that was there time after time as they look back on their lives. Oh if they only had one more chance . . .

But their chances are over and they have no more chances. All they can see is the darkness that is over at the place they now know they will be going to shortly. There seems to be something that they're getting whiffs of from time to time, and the stench that wafts up their noses is getting ever more frequent. It is a putrid and sulfuric smell and its intensity is making them nauseous.

These two destinies are comparable in quantity because they both are for the same enduring time . . . eternity. Yes my friend, the truth is, both these scenarios are for the same duration, but the comparison of the qualities of the lives lived in each place are so far apart, we have difficulty even putting the two side by side. The utter joy and the desperate torment and agony can hardly be put in the same sentence.

One is in hell for eternity and the other is in heaven for the same. The problem with unbelievers is, they won't be able to cross the divide between these two entities. Which side of this King will you be standing on? You'd best be ready because once you're placed on one side or the other, you're done!

Matthew 25:34-46 – "Then the King will say to those on His right, 'Come, you who are blessed of My Father, inherit the kingdom prepared for you from the foundation of the world. ³⁵ 'For I was hungry, and you gave Me *something* to eat; I was thirsty, and you gave Me drink; I was a stranger, and you invited Me in; ³⁶ naked, and you clothed Me; I was sick, and you visited Me; I was in prison, and you came to Me.' ³⁷ "Then the righteous will answer Him, saying, 'Lord, when did we see You hungry, and feed You, or thirsty, and give You drink? [38] 'And when did we see You a stranger, and invite You in, or naked, and clothe You? [39] 'And when did we see You sick, or in prison, and come to You?' [40] "And the King will answer and say to them, 'Truly I say to you, to the extent that you did it to one of these brothers of Mine, *even* the least *of them*, you did it to Me.' [41] "Then He will also say to those on His left, 'Depart from Me, accursed ones, into the eternal fire which has been prepared for the devil and his angels; [42] for I was hungry, and you gave Me *nothing* to eat; I was thirsty, and you gave Me nothing to drink; [43] I was a stranger, and you did not invite Me in; naked, and you did not clothe Me; sick, and in prison, and you did not visit Me.' [44] "Then they themselves also will answer, saying, 'Lord, when did we see You hungry, or thirsty, or a stranger, or naked, or sick, or in prison, and did not take care of You?' [45] "Then He will answer them, saying, 'Truly I say to you, to the extent that you did not do it to one of the least of these, you did not do it to Me.' [46] "And these will go away into eternal punishment, but the righteous into eternal life."

That was part of the problem with the King and Messiah Jesus Christ. He gave and allowed the freedom of decision, for men to do with Him as they pleased. He never forced Himself on anyone. But He did show mercy and grace to all He came in contact with. Jesus was there for all who wanted to come to Him and He showed love and respect to all. Even those who mocked and made fun of Him were asked to be forgiven by the God of the universe by the Man Jesus – the God of the universe. Imagine that . . . God asking for forgiveness for all those who persecute Him.

So here's Pilate, speaking to Jesus as a mere errand boy or a mosquito that he is ready to squash – not even knowing that THE GOD of the universe is WHO he is speaking to. Now wrap your brain around this – those who mock and despise Jesus Christ are spitting on the ONE who is actually praying for their salvation - even though they are spitting on HIM! AMAZING . . . isn't it?

John 18:37 – Pilate therefore said to Him, "So You are a king?" Jesus answered, "You say *correctly* that I am a king. For this I have been born, and for this I have come into the world, to bear witness to the truth. Everyone who is of the truth hears My voice."

Jesus Christ is the One Who loves us so, that He gave EVERYTHING, even His life, in order to save us from sin, death, and ourselves. He came to testify to the truth; the "absolute truth," that our society hates to admit is real. He was and still is, the One of perfect patience . . . not wanting any to perish. Otherwise He would have already exhibited His fury in avenging His Father's Holy Name from those who reject and show utter disrespect for Him.

1 Timothy 1:15-17 – It is a trustworthy statement, deserving full acceptance, that Christ Jesus came into the world to save sinners, among whom I am foremost *of all*. [16] And yet for this reason I found mercy, in order that in me as the foremost, Jesus Christ might demonstrate His perfect patience, as an example for those who would believe in Him for eternal life. [17] Now to the King eternal, immortal, invisible, the only God, *be* honor and glory forever and ever. Amen.

Jesus will come at the proper and perfect time of His Father's timing, in order to carry out the perfect plan. Christ and Christ alone has power over the lives of all and the earth they dwell on. His power over life and over death is unmatched and immeasurable.

> **1 Timothy 6:13-16 – I charge you in the presence of God, who gives life to all things, and of Christ Jesus, who testified the good confession before Pontius Pilate, [14] that you keep the commandment without stain or reproach until the appearing of our Lord Jesus Christ, [15] which He will bring about at the proper time – He who is the blessed and only Sovereign, the King of kings and Lord of lords; [16] who alone possesses immortality and dwells in unapproachable light; whom no man has seen or can see. To Him *be* honor and eternal dominion! Amen.**

War is coming and it is not the same type of war we are used to seeing. You know . . . the ones that we see on the news where it's all those people way over there who are involved. Everyone on the earth will be participating in this war in one way or another. It will be massive, cataclysmic, and catastrophic in nature. However, the war will be over before it is barely started, for there will be no match for the wondrous power of our Lord and Savior . . . the King of Kings.

> **Revelation 17:14 – "These will wage war against the Lamb, and the Lamb will overcome them, because He is Lord of lords and King of kings, and those who are with Him *are the* called and chosen and faithful."**

Yes this is the King we worship and the King Who truly

deserves that worship. How awesome He is and how awestruck we will be at the coming eternity He ushers in when the time is come. What a feast it will be for those who are believers in the One True God.

Revelation 19:5-16 – And a voice came from the throne, saying, "Give praise to our God, all you His bond-servants, you who fear Him, the small and the great." [6] And I heard, as it were, the voice of a great multitude and as the sound of many waters and as the sound of mighty peals of thunder, saying, "Hallelujah! For the Lord our God, the Almighty, reigns. [7] "Let us rejoice and be glad and give the glory to Him, for the marriage of the Lamb has come and His bride has made herself ready." [8] And it was given to her to clothe herself in fine linen, bright *and* clean; for the fine linen is the righteous acts of the saints. [9] And he said to me, "Write, 'Blessed are those who are invited to the marriage supper of the Lamb.'" And he said to me, "These are true words of God." [10] And I fell at his feet to worship him. And he said to me, "Do not do that; I am a fellow servant of yours and your brethren who hold the testimony of Jesus; worship God. For the testimony of Jesus is the spirit of prophecy." [11] And I saw heaven opened; and behold, a white horse, and He who sat upon it *is* called Faithful and True; and in righteousness He judges and wages war. [12] And His eyes *are* a flame of fire, and upon His head *are* many diadems; and He has a name written *upon Him* which no one knows except Himself. [13] And *He is* clothed with a robe dipped in blood; and His name is called The Word of God. [14] And the armies which are in heaven, clothed in fine linen, white *and* clean, were following Him on white horses. [15] And from His mouth comes a sharp sword, so that with it He may smite the nations; and He will rule them with a rod of iron; and He treads the wine press of the fierce wrath of God, the Almighty. [16] And on His robe and on His thigh He has a name written, "KING OF KINGS, AND LORD OF LORDS."

So this is my KING! Who is your king? You best make sure he is the "KING" with no other kings over him. It would be a sad and dreary day to realize the king one chooses is not really the king at all, but a mere "wannabe" king. One who has no power whatsoever to save and to protect those who worship him.

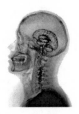

CHAPTER 11 – ?

What "FOUNDATION" will you build on? And just what "LEGACY" will you leave? Pondering questions such as these doesn't seem to come across most of our minds very often. Whether we have contemplated them or not, we each will leave an imprint on this earth and those around us in it. Will it be the imprint that the God of the universe wanted? Or will it be contrary to His plan that He had for our lives? We each get a choice you know.

Unfortunately most of us don't really even consider that we are impacting others for, or against Jesus Christ. Even if we don't believe that He is the Savior to the world, we still impact others to be drawn to Him . . . or away from Him. The sad reality is that this life will be over in a breath and we will each look back and wonder where the time has gone, with no way to possibly retrieve it.

Instead of thinking about the eternal ramifications of what we are striving to accomplish, we look to the immediate and short-lived benefits of taking care of ourselves, and our desires. We neglect and oftentimes totally ignore the truth of God and the eternal aspects of all of our decisions we make along the pathway of this life. By default, we engage and worship the temporary and fleeting, while our foundation we think is solid as a rock, turns out to be as the dust blown away by the wind or broken into pieces and crushed, perishing forever.

> Job 4:17-21 – 'Can mankind be just before God? Can a man be pure before his Maker? ¹⁸ 'He puts no trust even in His servants; And against His angels He charges error. ¹⁹ 'How much more those who dwell in houses of clay, Whose foundation is in the dust, Who are crushed before the moth! ²⁰ 'Between morning and evening they are broken in pieces; Unobserved, they perish forever. ²¹ 'Is not their tent-cord plucked up within them? They die, yet without wisdom.'

We tend to think that what we are doing is so very important and that the world can't do without our efforts. All the while we see with eyes glazed over and vision skewed that we can't even realize we are but specks on this tiny little globe among all the vastness of the universe. We take for granted that the God of truth holds the whole vast and wondrous universe we see around us in the palm of His hand.

Some of us think that global warming is what is determining the changes in the atmosphere and the environment around us. How arrogant and egotistical a notion it is – that as the inhabitants of this place we call earth, somehow we're in control of what happens on this micro- marble in the universe. Yes, we have no inkling what we are talking about, but we make these grandiose claims and fight for them tooth and nail as if the world's very existence depended on the outcome. All the while, God in His majestic and omnipotent truth watches over all our bumbling's and misfires at controlling and running something we have no clue how to live peaceably on, much less manage.

I heard someone once claim that the shorelines would change and the levels of the oceans would vary. Let's see what our God, the true God of the universe says about that comment . . .

Job 38:1-13 – Then the LORD answered Job out of the whirlwind and said, [2] "Who is this that darkens counsel By words without knowledge? [3] "Now gird up your loins like a man, And I will ask you, and you instruct Me! [4] "Where were you when I laid the foundation of the earth? Tell *Me*, if you have understanding, [5] Who set its measurements, since you know? Or who stretched the line on it? [6] "On what were its bases sunk? Or who laid its cornerstone, [7] When the morning stars sang together, And all the sons of God shouted for joy? [8] "Or *who* enclosed the sea with doors, When, bursting forth, it went out from the womb; [9] When I made a cloud its garment, And thick darkness its swaddling band, [10] And I placed boundaries on it, And I set a bolt and doors, [11] And I said, 'Thus far you shall come, but no farther; And here shall your proud waves stop '? [12] "Have you ever in your life commanded the morning, *And* caused the dawn to know its place; [13] That it might take hold of the ends of the earth, And the wicked be shaken out of it?

God alone is the One who can provide an everlasting true foundation for all of those who look to Him as their refuge. Jesus Christ's foundation is the only sure and lasting footing that we can place our trust and confidence in. We come to His sanctuary on His terms and by His means however. There is no faking and no illusion as to who will and who won't be admitted into His presence. The line will be drawn and it won't be one of those fuzzy and ambiguous lines either. The demarcation will be razor sharp.

> **Proverbs 10:22-25 – It is the blessing of the LORD that makes rich, And He adds no sorrow to it. ²³ Doing wickedness is like sport to a fool; And *so is* wisdom to a man of understanding. ²⁴ What the wicked fears will come upon him, And the desire of the righteous will be granted. ²⁵ When the whirlwind passes, the wicked is no more, But the righteous *has* an everlasting foundation.**

The Lord offers His rest to those who seek and diligently pursue Him. They are the ones who earnestly hunt and find His ways of growing them in their walks of faith. This faith is not some happenstance or quirky game that one slips and falls into. No, this relationship is established day by day, minute by minute, moment by moment as those who are brought into the kingdom are shaped, molded, and transformed more and more into the likeness of the Son of Man and Son of God through His indwelling Holy Spirit.

All along the way there will be those who scoff and ridicule Jesus Christ and His followers. The scoffers may have a time where they seem to have the upper hand, but the overwhelming scourge will one day have its reckoning and the place for doubt will be forever vanquished from the minds of all as to Who is really in charge and in control. The true foundation and cornerstone will be revealed and made evident for the eons of time to come.

> **Isaiah 28:10-18 – "For *He says*, 'Order on order, order on order, Line on line, line on line, A little here, a**

little there."' ¹¹ Indeed, He will speak to this people Through stammering lips and a foreign tongue, ¹² He who said to them, "Here is rest, give rest to the weary," And, "Here is repose," but they would not listen. ¹³ So the word of the LORD to them will be, "Order on order, order on order, Line on line, line on line, A little here, a little there," That they may go and stumble backward, be broken, snared, and taken captive. ¹⁴ Therefore, hear the word of the LORD, O scoffers, Who rule this people who are in Jerusalem, ¹⁵ Because you have said, "We have made a covenant with death, And with Sheol we have made a pact. The overwhelming scourge will not reach us when it passes by, For we have made falsehood our refuge and we have concealed ourselves with deception." ¹⁶ Therefore thus says the Lord God, "Behold, I am laying in Zion a stone, a tested stone, A costly cornerstone *for* the foundation, firmly placed. He who believes *in it* will not be disturbed. ¹⁷ "And I will make justice the measuring line, And righteousness the level; Then hail shall sweep away the refuge of lies, And the waters shall overflow the secret place. ¹⁸ "And your covenant with death shall be canceled, And your pact with Sheol shall not stand; When the overwhelming scourge passes through, Then you become its trampling *place.*

Those who have misled the people will come to a violent and rightful end in which the wrath of the holy God will find them out and take them down to the pits of hell. They will have chosen to build on the wrong and false foundation and they will find that they have not put their faith in the costly cornerstone, Jesus Christ. They will find their lot has been cast with the father of lies . . . Satan. And it will be too late to retrieve their souls from eternal torment.

> **Ezekiel 13:9-17 –** "So My hand will be against the prophets who see false visions and utter lying divinations. They will have no place in the council of My people, nor will they be written down in the register of the house of Israel, nor will they enter the land of Israel, that you may know that I am the Lord God. [10] "It is definitely because they have misled My people by saying, 'Peace!' when there is no peace. And when anyone builds a wall, behold, they plaster it over with whitewash; [11] *so* tell those who plaster it over with whitewash, that it will fall. A flooding rain will come, and you, O hailstones, will fall; and a violent wind will break out. [12] "Behold, when the wall has fallen, will you not be asked, 'Where is the plaster with which you plastered *it*?'" [13] Therefore, thus says the Lord God, "I will make a violent wind break out in My wrath. There will also be in My anger a flooding rain and hailstones to consume *it* in wrath. [14] "So I shall tear down the wall which you plastered over with whitewash and bring it down to the ground, so that its foundation is laid bare; and when it falls, you will be consumed in its midst. And you will know that I am the LORD. [15] "Thus I shall spend My wrath on the wall and on those who have plastered it over with whitewash; and I shall say to you, 'The wall is gone and its plasterers are gone, [16] *along with* the prophets of Israel who prophesy to Jerusalem, and who see visions of peace for her when there is no peace,' declares the Lord God. [17] "Now you, son of man, set your face against

the daughters of your people who are prophesying from their own inspiration. Prophesy against them,

The ones who have relied on their own power and strength will find that they relied on the wrong idol . . . themselves. The blessed Holy Spirit is the power on which anything of true value is brought about. All else will be seen for what it really is; wasted time and wasted effort that was centered on self. The Lord will know what is true and what is false. After all, He is God, and all the true and good that comes about will be by His Holy Spirit.

Zechariah 4:6 – Then he answered and said to me, "This is the word of the LORD to Zerubbabel saying, 'Not by might nor by power, but by My Spirit,' says the LORD of hosts.

So again we should be asking ourselves . . ." what foundation will I be building on? What legacy will I leave?" We had better be discerning about who we hang out with and listen to. And we had better be careful how we build, for how we build will follow us throughout eternity.

We are the ones who will answer for our efforts to raise our kids in a Godly home centered on Jesus Christ . . . or not. A lot of the significance of the foundation we build on is revealed in how our family and kids turn out. Who do they worship and spend their time seeking? What impact will they have on all those they come in contact with in the world around them?

No doubt there are those parents who raised their kids in a strong Christian environment, only to watch those kids make poor decision after poor decision, that lead to the heartache of all concerned. Or Christian families who have kids that start out so promising in their faith, but then get off-track and spiral out of control. This life has no guarantees of success, even for those families earnestly seeking our Savior.

What type of marriage will our kids have, and how will we help to train them. Will they respect their spouse and learn to serve them, instead of only looking out for themselves? How can we help them maintain their relationship with Jesus Christ through prayer and the study of His Word, so they're enabled to love their spouse with the love of Christ? Will they have the stick-to-it-iveness to stay with their marriage when the times are tough, so they're enabled to have a chance to grow with their life partner in order to have a melding of their hearts into one flesh?

Or will they be looking for the wrong things in the spouse they choose? I've heard story after story of the son or daughter who looked for and found what the world said was the best partner for them; good looks, great job, excellent income and a beautiful home. It seemed everything was perfect . . . for a while. Then it finally dawns on them that the one they picked was selfish and had no consideration for the partner they married – all the while claiming to be a devout and dedicated Christian.

Or the other common theme where the son or daughter who seemed so strong in their faith falls for someone who has no faith at all. Such people often believe they'll be able to change their spouse and bring them to Jesus Christ. This reminds me of a time that a mentor told me "Mark, you can change people . . . just not very much!" It is a lie that we think we can change people, and we tell ourselves all too often. Don't think that you can change others into what you want them to be. Only God, through His Holy Spirit, can change people . . . meaningfully.

If parents aren't making good decisions in life, neither will their kids. Digging deep into our faith in Christ will take effort, but the results will be well worth that effort down the line . . . in eternity. Of course, this isn't in sync with our "immediate gratification" culture that we are so enmeshed in today.

Likewise, the lack of effort in seeking Christ will result in more heartache than we can possibly imagine. We will have the dubious opportunity of watching our mistakes repeated and compounded over and over, recurring in the adverse ways our kids and grandkids live their lives with all the poor decisions they are making. Guess where they learned how to make those poor decisions?

Luke 6:47-49 – "Everyone who comes to Me, and hears My words, and acts upon them, I will show you whom he is like: [48] he is like a man building a house, who dug deep and laid a foundation upon the rock; and when a flood rose, the torrent burst against that house and could not shake it, because it had been well built. [49] "But the one who has heard, and has not acted *accordingly*, is like a man who built a house upon the ground without any foundation; and the torrent burst against it and immediately it collapsed, and the ruin of that house was great."

Some call **John 17** the "Holy of Holies". It's the place in the Bible where Jesus prays for those who call Him their Lord and Savior. Jesus prays to His Father in heaven mainly for those of us who believe in Him. Jesus wants our sanctification and He wants us to have ultimate joy with He and His Father. Even though He knows that the world will hate those who follow Him, He wants them to know His joy that passes all understanding for those who are faithful to stay their faith in Him.

John 17:12-26 – "While I was with them, I was keeping them in Thy name which Thou hast given Me; and I guarded them, and not one of them perished but the son of perdition, that the Scripture might be fulfilled. [13] "But now I come to Thee; and these things I speak in the world, that they may have My joy made full in themselves. [14] "I have given them Thy word; and the world has hated them, because they are not of the world, even as I am not of the world. [15] "I do not ask Thee to take them out of the world, but to keep them from the evil *one*. [16] "They are not of the world, even as I am not of the world. [17] "Sanctify them in the truth; Thy word is truth. [18] "As Thou didst send Me into the world, I also have sent them into the world. [19] "And for their sakes I sanctify Myself, that they themselves also may be sanctified in truth. [20] "I do not ask in behalf of these alone, but for those also who believe in Me through their word; [21] that they may all be one; even as Thou, Father, *art* in Me, and I in Thee, that they also may be in Us; that the world may believe that Thou didst send Me. [22] "And the glory which Thou hast given Me I have given to them; that they may be one, just as We are one; [23] I in them, and Thou in Me, that they may be perfected in unity, that the world may know that Thou didst send Me, and didst love them, even as Thou didst love Me. [24] "Father, I desire that they also, whom Thou hast given Me, be with Me where I am, in order that they may behold My glory, which Thou hast given Me; for Thou didst love Me before the foundation of the world. [25] "O righteous Father, although the world has not known Thee, yet I have known Thee; and these have known that Thou didst send Me; [26] and I have made Thy name known to them,

and will make it known; that the love wherewith Thou didst love Me may be in them, and I in them."

I've gotten together with two mentors in the last week and reconnected with an old acquaintance from college days as well. If you don't mind I'd like to share with you the three of these men's comments from our conversations. The first was a breakfast meeting with a gentleman who had just finished reading my first book a few days before. He is a very learned man with many degrees, a prestigious position at a large company, and on the verge of going after another graduate degree at a prominent seminary. He is focused and committed in his involvement in his church, as well as in his daily walk with our Savior.

He made a comment about what he got out of the book that stopped me in my tracks . . . He said, "You know Mark, what I got out of your book is that on my walk of faith with Christ . . . I need to be more intentional in sharing my faith with those around me on a daily basis . . ."

Wow! You could have knocked me over with a feather! Seriously??? It seemed like one of those AHA!!! . . . moments. Here is a man who has spent untold hours in serving our Lord and Savior for decades; spending time in God's Word, in prayer, in service, and in relationship with Christ the true King. Even with all that time and effort, he still feels that he has not shared his faith with those around him as much as he should have – and that he's been missing opportunities to impact others for Christ.

The second instance is the reconnecting with an old college acquaintance from West Texas. He had sent out an email notifying me that a friend of ours is battling pancreatic cancer. I gave him a call back to check on our friend and we agreed to reconnect sometime soon.

He called a couple of days later and we spent over an hour and a half on the phone catching up on our lives, other friends, and what had happened to all of us through the years. Our conversation turned to our walks of faith within the first thirty minutes and never left that topic for the next hour. He spoke of his involvement with a Christian retreat ministry called the Walk to Emmaus, and how he has been involved with this great ministry as an organizer and speaker for the last fifteen years. I mentioned to him that I had gone on a "walk" twenty one years ago while Keyea was pregnant with Kailey, and that it was a true "mountain top" experience on my walk of faith.

While all our conversation was very meaningful and encouraging, one comment he made really stuck with me. He said, "Mark, I've got one last financial goal that I'm going to accomplish real soon . . . like in the next two years. When I've got that done, I want to settle down and do something that really makes a difference in this world . . . you know something that really makes an impact on those around me on their walk of faith."

There it was again . . . someone wanting to make a difference in the walks of faith in Christ of those around them.

The third encounter was a lunch with another mentor. This man has been dedicated to his study of God's Word again – for decades. He has written several books, and continues to write more commentaries on books of the Bible, as well as Q&A's for believers to better understand how to walk more closely with Christ.

As we sat there, he told me that he had a thought when he was arising from a nap and still in a fog. He said to himself, "Have I done anything for my Savior that has truly been 'relevant?'" Are you seeing a pattern appearing in these paragraphs? It is a question and contemplation we all come to grips with at some point in our lives – "Has my life had any real impact and meaning in this world I'm living in?"

I asked him if he still had any copies of one of the books he had written that had impacted me. He said, "Yes Mark, I've got some of them left." I commented to him, "One thing I can tell you is this – that book was pivotal in my life and in my walk of faith. It impacted me in a profound way and actually helped me to realize that I needed to get my family to another church home." He looked at me and smiled, "You know, that might have been the reason the Lord had me write it, Mark."

I'm sure his book has impacted others on their walks of faith as well, but one thing is sure in my mind . . . I needed to read what he wrote in that book. It spoke to me about what was going on in my previous church, and enabled me to see that the Lord wanted me and my family to move on to another one. Reading that book has been huge in my growth of faith, and my family's faith also. In fact, in a round-a-bout way . . . it led to my writing *Which Way Is Up?*.

So what is the "common thread" amongst these three men of high integrity and strong dedicated faith in our Savior? It is this: No matter how much time we spend with Christ in prayer and in His Word, how much time we spend in conversation with others about their walks of faith, or how many people the Lord may enable us to have an impact on for Him...we all know that it is not even a drop in the bucket compared to the ultimate sacrifice borne by our Lord and Savior for our redemption. The result is, we want to do more and even more for Christ and His kingdom.

All three of these men have been impacting people for Christ for decades . . . and they all three know that through Christ and His indwelling Holy Spirit they can do more! And we can too, if we will admit it to ourselves, and be "sold-out" for the gospel of Jesus Christ. Yes, we must be careful how we build on the true foundation that God gives us to build on. It must be His foundation and not our own, and it must be the "Rock" of the foundation of Jesus Christ – for there is no other.

> 1 Corinthians 3:10-23 – According to the grace of God which was given to me, as a wise master builder I laid a foundation, and another is building upon it. But let each man be careful how he builds upon it. [11] For no man can lay a foundation other than the one which is laid, which is Jesus Christ. [12] Now if any man builds upon the foundation with gold, silver, precious stones, wood, hay, straw, [13] each man's work will become evident; for the day will show it, because it is *to be* revealed with fire; and the fire itself will test the quality of each man's work. [14] If any man's work which he has built upon it remains, he shall receive a reward. [15] If any man's work is burned up, he shall suffer loss; but he himself shall be saved, yet so as through fire. [16] Do you not know that you are a temple of God, and *that* the Spirit of God dwells in you? [17] If any man destroys the temple of God, God will destroy him, for the temple of God is holy, and that is what you are. [18] Let no man deceive himself. If any man among you thinks that he is wise in this age, let him become foolish that he may become wise. [19] For the wisdom of this world is foolishness before God. For it is written, "*He is* the one who catches the wise in their craftiness"; [20] and again, "The Lord knows the reasonings of the wise, that they are useless." [21] So then let no one boast in men. For all things belong to you, [22] whether Paul or Apollos or Cephas or the

world or life or death or things present or things to
come; all things belong to you, [23] and you belong to
Christ; and Christ belongs to God.

Yes we all must be careful how we build because what we
build upon follows us for eternity . . . that is unless it is "burnt
up." Most of what we pursue is temporal and not lasting. Isn't
it a shame . . . that we put so much effort into the fleeting
and perishing, rather than into the eternal and lasting work
of Jesus Christ?

And isn't it amazing that we can discount what God says
as irrelevant and not important, when in reality, His Word of
truth and our relationship with Him through that Word and
prayer is the most important endeavor we could possibly be
involved in? Instead we remind ourselves, "Oh well, there it
goes . . . another day without spending time with my Savior.
One of these days I'll figure out how to make the time to
spend with Him . . ."

So are we all idiots? Some say it's a given! We are caught
up in our seeming craftiness, with no inkling as to what true
wisdom is. But wait – there is hope. Even though we may feel
we are far off from our Lord and Savior, there is the hope that
He is there for us sinners and we can return to Him even now.
In fact, we can be brought back into peace and reconciliation
with our Redeemer for eternity.

Ephesians 2:13-22 – But now in Christ Jesus you
who formerly were far off have been brought near by
the blood of Christ. [14] For He Himself is our peace,
who made both *groups into* one, and broke down the
barrier of the dividing wall, [15] by abolishing in His
flesh the enmity, *which is* the Law of commandments
contained in ordinances, that in Himself He might

make the two into one new man, *thus* establishing peace, [16] and might reconcile them both in one body to God through the cross, by it having put to death the enmity. [17] And He came and preached peace to you who were far away, and peace to those who were near; [18] for through Him we both have our access in one Spirit to the Father. [19] So then you are no longer strangers and aliens, but you are fellow citizens with the saints, and are of God's household, [20] having been built upon the foundation of the apostles and prophets, Christ Jesus Himself being the corner *stone*, [21] in whom the whole building, being fitted together is growing into a holy temple in the Lord; [22] in whom you also are being built together into a dwelling of God in the Spirit.

Having been reconciled through the Holy Spirit, we can fight the good fight of faith. Are you ready to do so? Can you see that the God of the universe is calling you to the purpose that He has for your life? Take hold of Christ and earnestly seek Him. You won't be sorry that you did. He will enable you to live the life you never dreamed you could live with the results you never imagined could be accomplished. Realize that the riches of this world are but refuse and have no real lasting value when Christ returns to bring us home to be with Him in heaven.

1 Timothy 6:12-21 – Fight the good fight of faith; take hold of the eternal life to which you were called, and you made the good confession in the presence of many witnesses. [13] I charge you in the presence of God, who gives life to all things, and of Christ Jesus, who testified the good confession before Pontius Pilate, [14] that you keep the commandment without stain or reproach

until the appearing of our Lord Jesus Christ, [15] which He will bring about at the proper time – He who is the blessed and only Sovereign, the King of kings and Lord of lords; [16] who alone possesses immortality and dwells in unapproachable light; whom no man has seen or can see. To Him *be* honor and eternal dominion! Amen. [17] Instruct those who are rich in this present world not to be conceited or to fix their hope on the uncertainty of riches, but on God, who richly supplies us with all things to enjoy. [18] *Instruct them* to do good, to be rich in good works, to be generous and ready to share, [19] storing up for themselves the treasure of a good foundation for the future, so that they may take hold of that which is life indeed. [20] O Timothy, guard what has been entrusted to you, avoiding worldly *and* empty chatter *and* the opposing arguments of what is falsely called "knowledge" – [21] which some have professed and thus gone astray from the faith. Grace be with you.

The Lord will help us to not be the lost sheep anymore. Though we have strayed in the past, we now know Christ the King of all Kings and the Lord of all Lords. And guess what? He knows us as well, and He will help us to know Him even more intimately and will enable us to abstain from the wickedness that perverts this world around us!

2 Timothy 2:19 – Nevertheless, the firm foundation of God stands, having this seal, "The Lord knows those who are His," and, "Let everyone who names the name of the Lord abstain from wickedness."

Thus He will make us to shine like lights in the darkness, revealing Him to those whose eyes have been clouded with the chaos of this world. And He will enable us to partake in His wonderful and perfect plan of redemption; ministering and witnessing to those He sends across our paths in this world. We will then be ministers of the light of Christ, helping others to escape the darkness so prevalent in this world we now live in.

> Acts 26:15-18 – "And I said, 'Who art Thou, Lord?' And the Lord said, 'I am Jesus whom you are persecuting. [16] 'But arise, and stand on your feet; for this purpose I have appeared to you, to appoint you a minister and a witness not only to the things which you have seen, but also to the things in which I will appear to you; [17] delivering you from the *Jewish* people and from the Gentiles, to whom I am sending you, [18] to open their eyes so that they may turn from darkness to light and from the dominion of Satan to God, in order that they may receive forgiveness of sins and an inheritance among those who have been sanctified by faith in Me.'

This opening of our own eyes will then allow us to be better stewards of our own families and households. We will have the where-with-all to stand firm for our Savior and for our faith. We will reclaim our families and reassert ourselves to the task of building our family members up in Christ . . . or we will not. The choice is always there. We can refuse to make the effort and build on the strong foundation of Jesus Christ. We can choose to wing-it and go our own way . . . turning our backs on the only Savior Who would love to save us. After all, He and his followers all appear so weak.

My friend, don't kid yourself. Never think that Jesus Christ and His followers are weak. They are anything but. Choosing to serve and follow Christ is not for the faint of heart. There is serious work to be done to further His kingdom and draw others to Him. At times the work can appear to be overwhelming and unachievable, but He gives those who earnestly seek Him the power to overcome the most formidable obstacles imaginable. Earnestly seek Him and He will give you the true happiness and meaningful life that you never even knew could exist this side of heaven.

We all want to provide for our kids to have the best life they possibly can. Those of us that are parents want to do the best we can for our kids, so what do you think our Lord and Savior wants to do for us? He wants to provide the most meaningful and fulfilling life that we can possibly have for His kingdom. Christ is not concerned about giving us worldly stuff to make us comfortable, but He does want to give us the things that are necessary to help us to "press-on" and impact those around us in a mighty way for the right reason . . . His glory. There is no gift greater than His indwelling Holy Spirit to fill us and guide us on the path He gives us to take.

Luke 11:13 – "If you then, being evil, know how to give good gifts to your children, how much more shall *your* heavenly Father give the Holy Spirit to those who ask Him?"

I said this in my first book, but I think it bears repeating . . . Sanctification is a process, and holiness a destination. That is a true statement wouldn't you say? Our walk of faith is a process, and yes there is a destination. The problem we need to realize is that that destination is only accomplished by the shed blood of Jesus Christ and the indwelling of the Holy Spirit. If we choose Christ and seek Him diligently, He will faithfully persevere to sanctify us entirely. However, we must spend time with Him. Both in prayer and in His true Word.

1 Thessalonians 5:23-24 – Now may the God of peace Himself sanctify you entirely; and may your spirit and soul and body be preserved complete, without blame at the coming of our Lord Jesus Christ. ²⁴ Faithful is He who calls you, and He also will bring it to pass.

Christ alone has the perfect righteousness and holiness for the perfect foundation that only He can provide. His adversaries have no hope, so either you are against Him – lost and defeated and doomed to total separation from God for eternity – or you are with Him and victorious, and will see His glory manifested for eternity in heaven above.

Psalm 97:1-12 – The LORD reigns; let the earth rejoice; Let the many islands be glad. ² Clouds and thick darkness surround Him; Righteousness and justice are the foundation of His throne. ³ Fire goes before Him, And burns up His adversaries round about. ⁴ His lightnings lit up the world; The earth saw and trembled. ⁵ The mountains melted like wax at the presence of the LORD, At the presence of the Lord of the whole earth. ⁶ The heavens declare His righteousness, And all the peoples have seen His glory. ⁷ Let all those be ashamed who serve graven images, Who boast themselves of idols; Worship Him, all you gods. ⁸ Zion heard *this* and was glad, And the daughters of Judah have rejoiced Because of Thy judgments, O LORD. ⁹ For Thou art the LORD Most High over all the earth; Thou art exalted far above all gods. ¹⁰ Hate evil, you who love the LORD, Who preserves the souls of His godly ones; He delivers them from the hand of the wicked. ¹¹ Light is sown *like seed* for the righteous, And gladness for the upright in heart. ¹² Be glad in

the LORD, you righteous ones; And give thanks to His holy name.

Then the glory and honor of the Father of the universe will lay claim in wondrous raiment for all those reconciled and redeemed forever to see. The beautiful city will be revealed and the true foundation that lasts eternally will be laid and visible for the believers to see.

Revelation 21:14-27 – And the wall of the city had twelve foundation stones, and on them *were* the twelve names of the twelve apostles of the Lamb. [15] And the one who spoke with me had a gold measuring rod to measure the city, and its gates and its wall. [16] And the city is laid out as a square, and its length is as great as the width; and he measured the city with the rod, fifteen hundred miles; its length and width and height are equal. [17] And he measured its wall, seventy-two yards, *according to* human measurements, which are *also* angelic *measurements*. [18] And the material of the wall was jasper; and the city was pure gold, like clear glass. [19] The foundation stones of the city wall were adorned with every kind of precious stone. The first foundation stone was jasper; the second, sapphire; the third, chalcedony; the fourth, emerald; [20] the fifth, sardonyx; the sixth, sardius; the seventh, chrysolite; the eighth, beryl; the ninth, topaz; the tenth, chrysoprase; the eleventh, jacinth; the twelfth, amethyst. [21] And the twelve gates were twelve pearls; each one of the gates was a single pearl. And the street of the city was pure gold, like transparent glass. [22] And I saw no temple in it, for the Lord God, the Almighty, and the Lamb, are its temple.

²³ And the city has no need of the sun or of the moon to shine upon it, for the glory of God has illumined it, and its lamp *is* the Lamb. ²⁴ And the nations shall walk by its light, and the kings of the earth shall bring their glory into it. ²⁵ And in the daytime (for there shall be no night there) its gates shall never be closed; ²⁶ and they shall bring the glory and the honor of the nations into it; ²⁷ and nothing unclean and no one who practices abomination and lying, shall ever come into it, but only those whose names are written in the Lamb's book of life.

Then the legacies and true foundation of the Lord Jesus Christ will be there for all the Cosmos to look down on and finally understand that God's plan was and is indeed PERFECT! There won't be any hesitation and there won't be any doubt that God is the great "I AM!" and worthy of that name above all names. The name that every knee will bow to. The perfection of God's plan will be manifest, showing how His Word – both the Old and the New Testaments – point to Jesus Christ as the Lord and Savior for all who believe. Jesus is the fulfillment of the Holy Scriptures, as well as the culmination of the first and new covenant provided by a loving and holy God. Christ alone obtains our eternal redemption through His shed blood on the cross.

Hebrews 9:1-28 – Now even the first *covenant* had regulations of divine worship and the earthly sanctuary. ² For there was a tabernacle prepared, the outer one, in which *were* the lampstand and the table and the sacred bread; this is called the holy place. ³ And behind the second veil, there was a tabernacle which is called the Holy of Holies, ⁴ having a golden altar of incense and the ark of the covenant covered on all sides with gold, in which *was* a golden jar holding the manna, and Aaron's rod which budded, and the tables of the covenant. [5] And above it *were* the cherubim of glory overshadowing the mercy seat; but of these things we cannot now speak in detail. [6] Now when these things have been thus prepared, the priests are continually entering the outer tabernacle, performing the divine worship, [7] but into the second only the high priest *enters*, once a year, not without *taking* blood, which he offers for himself and for the sins of the people committed in ignorance. [8] The Holy Spirit *is* signifying this, that the way into the holy place has not yet been disclosed, while the outer tabernacle is still standing, [9] which *is* a symbol for the present time. Accordingly both gifts and sacrifices are offered which cannot make the worshiper perfect in conscience, [10] since they *relate* only to food and drink and various washings, regulations for the body imposed until a time of reformation. [11] But when Christ appeared *as* a high priest of the good things to come, *He entered* through the greater and more perfect tabernacle, not made with hands, that is to say, not of this creation; [12] and not through the blood of goats and calves, but through His own blood, He entered the holy place once for all, having obtained eternal redemption. [13] For if the blood of goats and bulls and the ashes of a heifer sprinkling those who have been defiled, sanctify for the cleansing of the flesh, [14] how much more will the blood of Christ, who through the eternal Spirit offered Himself without blemish to God, cleanse your conscience from dead works to serve the living God? [15] And for this reason

He is the mediator of a new covenant, in order that since a death has taken place for the redemption of the transgressions that were *committed* under the first covenant, those who have been called may receive the promise of the eternal inheritance. [16] For where a covenant is, there must of necessity be the death of the one who made it. [17] For a covenant is valid *only* when men are dead, for it is never in force while the one who made it lives. [18] Therefore even the first *covenant* was not inaugurated without blood. [19] For when every commandment had been spoken by Moses to all the people according to the Law, he took the blood of the calves and the goats, with water and scarlet wool and hyssop, and sprinkled both the book itself and all the people, [20] saying, "This is the blood of the covenant which God commanded you." [21] And in the same way he sprinkled both the tabernacle and all the vessels of the ministry with the blood. [22] And according to the Law, *one may* almost *say*, all things are cleansed with blood, and without shedding of blood there is no forgiveness. [23] Therefore it was necessary for the copies of the things in the heavens to be cleansed with these, but the heavenly things themselves with better sacrifices than these. [24] For Christ did not enter a holy place made with hands, a *mere* copy of the true one, but into heaven itself, now to appear in the presence of God for us; [25] nor was it that He should offer Himself often, as the high priest enters the holy place year by year with blood not his own. [26] Otherwise, He would have needed to suffer often since the foundation of the world; but now once at the consummation of the ages He has been manifested to put away sin by the sacrifice of Himself. [27] And inasmuch as it is

appointed for men to die once and after this *comes* judgment, [28] so Christ also, having been offered once to bear the sins of many, shall appear a second time for salvation without *reference to* sin, to those who eagerly await Him.

Yes, Jesus Christ fulfilled all of the prophecies of the Old Testament, fulfilled all the wishes and commands of His Father in heaven, fulfilled all righteousness, and fulfilled the new covenant by living a perfectly sinless life on earth; He then sacrificed Himself on the cross in payment for our sins. Thus, He was and is the perfect and atoning sacrifice, without which we sinners could not be reconciled to God. He is the mediator of that new covenant while sitting at the right hand of His Father in heaven. He gives the lasting covenant that only He can provide for those who believe in His Holy name. Christ alone is the true foundation and He alone has the one and only true legacy for the ages.

I was asked recently to give a talk at a local college to a World Religion Class. The class had about twenty people in it, all of various and different religions. I would say the median age was around fifty five to sixty years of age. The class appeared to be organized in order to have an environment to hear about differing religions from various speakers sharing about their particular faiths.

I titled my talk . . . "Place Your Bets." At the beginning I asked these rhetorical questions . . .

- Do you believe that there is a heaven?
- Do you believe there is a hell?
- Do you want to spend eternity in heaven?
- If you died today, where would you be tomorrow?

- Why would you be there?
- Are you absolutely sure?
- Is there such a thing as absolute truth?
- Do you believe it?
- Do all roads of faith lead to heaven?

After going through these questions, I proceeded to give my testimony, give a statement of what I believe as a Christian, and then spoke on the verses from **Luke 18:9-14**. In these verses Jesus speaks about two men who went up to the temple to pray, one a Pharisee and the other a tax collector . . .

> **Luke 18:9-14 – And He also told this parable to certain ones who trusted in themselves that they were righteous, and viewed others with contempt:** [10] **"Two men went up into the temple to pray, one a Pharisee, and the other a tax-gatherer.** [11] **"The Pharisee stood and was praying thus to himself, 'God, I thank Thee that I am not like other people: swindlers, unjust, adulterers, or even like this tax-gatherer.** [12] **'I fast twice a week; I pay tithes of all that I get.'** [13] **"But the tax-gatherer, standing some distance away, was even unwilling to lift up his eyes to heaven, but was beating his breast, saying, 'God, be merciful to me, the sinner!'** [14] **"I tell you, this man went down to his house justified rather than the other; for everyone who exalts himself shall be humbled, but he who humbles himself shall be exalted."**

In these verses, Jesus seems to be giving us a comparison of those who realize their sinfulness and have faith in Him and

His saving grace contrasted with all other religions, which teach that man can "earn" his way to heaven.

Jesus speaks of those whose faith teaches them that they can be good enough and do enough good works to "force" God to humble Himself. And by their being "so very good", they force God's hand to receive them into heaven. This is basically what all other religions in the world besides Christianity teach: that through their own human achievement, people can earn their way to heaven. The Pharisee was doing this when he was speaking of all his good works. You know one thing he didn't express at all was that he had any "needs." Do you know why? It was because he felt he was good enough and self-righteous enough through his own "human achievement" that he didn't have any needs. He would earn his way to heaven on his own merits.

On the other hand, Jesus speaks of the despised tax collector, who having realized his own brokenness and sin, reaches outside of himself to the loving God and Savior Jesus Christ. The tax collector understands that he has no chance of being good enough to enter into heaven, and instead, throws himself at the foot of the cross of Christ and begs for his Savior to save him. You see, he realizes that in and of himself, he is destitute and lost in his sin. But when he comes to Christ, Jesus lovingly reaches out His hand to redeem this sinner, and clothe him in His righteousness for eternity.

Which of these two will you emulate in your walk of faith? Will you stand on your own works and merits to get you into heaven as the proud Pharisee did? Only to realize when it's too late that you come up short of the holiness that God the Father requires?

Or will you place your faith in the one and only perfect sacrificial Lamb of God, Jesus Christ, Who's atoning blood can wash your sins away and separate you from those sins as far as the east is from the west? Christ will thus impart His righteous holiness to you as a gift making you a fellow heir with Him in heaven!

> **2 Corinthians 5:17-21 – Therefore if any man is in Christ,** *he is* **a new creature; the old things passed away; behold, new things have come. ¹⁸ Now all** *these* **things are from God, who reconciled us to Himself through Christ, and gave us the ministry of reconciliation, ¹⁹ namely, that God was in Christ reconciling the world to Himself, not counting their trespasses against them, and He has committed to us the word of reconciliation. ²⁰ Therefore, we are ambassadors for Christ, as though God were entreating through us; we beg you on behalf of Christ, be reconciled to God. ²¹ He made Him who knew no sin** *to be* **sin on our behalf, that we might become the righteousness of God in Him.**

As we all live this life here on earth, we are all provided ample opportunities to come to a saving faith in Jesus Christ. What will you put your faith in? After all, we are each "PLACING OUR BETS!" – as to what we will believe in for each of our salvation. Just remember . . . you are betting your eternity on whoever or whatever you put your faith and trust in!

Will you and I be a part of Christ's "LEGACY"? Will we be standing firm on the one true "FOUNDATION" of Jesus Christ? He gives us a choice . . . and we must choose carefully! We wouldn't want to be "IDIOTS" would we?

In conclusion, I wouldn't say that all men and women are "IDIOTS." I would say that all of us are sinners! We're all lost like the sheep that Jesus speaks of in His Holy and True Word.

Would you like to be found? Would you like to change the path you are on? Would you like to have a positive change for you and your family? Who knows that change may even extend to your friends and coworkers around you? It can happen you know . . .

If you will humble yourself and come to Jesus Christ as your Lord and Savior, He will change you through His Holy Spirit. Accept His free gift of Himself along with His grace and payment for your sins. Then watch as the "FOUNDATION" you build on is strengthened and brought into play in every area and in every relationship you have. Once you belong to Him, the "LEGACY" you build will be changed and brought under the ultimate "LEGACY" of Jesus Christ . . . for eternity!

This is my prayer for you . . .

Colossians 1:9-14 – For this reason also, since the day we heard *of it*, we have not ceased to pray for you and to ask that you may be filled with the knowledge of His will in all spiritual wisdom and understanding, [10] so that you may walk in a manner worthy of the Lord, to please *Him* in all respects, bearing fruit in every good work and increasing in the knowledge of God; [11] strengthened with all power, according to His glorious might, for the attaining of all steadfastness and patience; joyously [12] giving thanks to the Father, who has qualified us to share in the inheritance of the saints in light. [13] For He delivered us from the domain of darkness, and transferred us to the kingdom of His beloved Son, [14] in whom we have redemption, the forgiveness of sins.

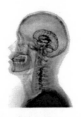

STUDY GUIDE

Chapter 1 – ALL

1. Where & when did "All Men Are Idiots" start?

2. Have you ever considered that God has a purpose for your life, and the life of your family?

3. How is Satan waging war on our families?

4. Why do you think God formed Eve out of Adam's rib?

5. How are humans sinners? Or wise?

6. Are couples who become "one flesh" dwindling?

7. Are you ready to stand in front of God . . . all by yourself?

8. Are you ashamed of Jesus Christ?

Chapter 2 – MEN

1. Do you agree that women are found wanting in wisdom as well as men?

2. Do you consider God's Word in helping you to make decisions? Or do you, "Do it my way?"

3. Do you feel we Americans are "choking on our blessings?"

4. Are you spending time daily in prayer and Bible study?

5. Are you accountable for your actions, or a victim of circumstances?

6. Are you and your spouse training up your kids in their walk of faith?

7. Who is the spiritual leader of your family?

8. Are you setting good examples for your kids to follow?

Chapter 3 – ARE

1. Do you covet what others have?

2. Does the grass appear greener on the other side in any areas in your life?

3. When will you be happy?

4. Do your sinful desires rob you of true happiness?

5. Does God keep your attention, or worldly things? How does it show?

6. Are you being transformed more and more into the likeness of Christ?

7. Are you choosing good friends?

8. Do you think God has a purpose for your life?

Chapter 4 – IDIOTS

1. Do you know anyone who is too smart for their own good?

2. Do you ignore God's instruction book – the Bible?

3. Are you sacrificing your family or kids on the altar of organized sports? Or anything else?

4. Are you helping your kids to set their focus on Jesus Christ?

5. Will your kids be trained up to be able to maintain their faith on into college?

6. Do you believe Jesus Christ is God? Or just a very good man?

7. Which is better . . . book smarts? Or wisdom from God's true Word?

8. Are you "wise" or "foolish" in your choices?

Chapter 5 – !

1. Who do you know that craves attention . . . do you do so?

2. How have we gotten lax in using our judgment to discern right from wrong?

3. How is Satan "loosening the stops" – to bring the family unit to its knees?

4. What is a "normal" family?

5. Do you Dad – "know the program" of being the spiritual leader of your family?

6. Who is raising our kids . . . the parents? . . . the Daycare centers? . . . TV? . . . social media?

7. How are you training up your kids in theBible?

8. What are you emphasizing to your kids?

Chapter 6 – AND

1. How are you anxious and worried about things?

2. Do you ever feel you are functioning just below the "panic level"?

3. How is there a "battle for your mind" going on?

4. What kind of pain and heartache do you see around you?

5. Do you believe that human beings are basically good?

6. Do you take any opportunities to give others Bibles or other helpful reading materials?

7. Do you give "lip service" to God? Or do you earnestly seek Him?

8. Are you "God-centered" and "other-centered" or "self-centered?"

Chapter 7 – I

1. Are you in an "I Coma"?

2. Do you, both men and women, see the "magic" that your spouse provides in your home?

3. Are you "stagnant" in Spirit?

4. How are you "dying to self" for Jesus' sake?

5. How are you bolder in sharing Christ and His gospel with those around you?

6. Are you looking for God's plan for your life? Or carrying out your own plan?

7. Does Christ have your focus? Or the world?

8. Are you available? And is God sending you out?

Chapter 8 – MARRIED

1. How is the judiciary dictating the Country's stance on marriage?

2. How do you feel about God's design for marriage as laid out in Genesis?

3. How is social media helping or hurting marriages?

4. Should couples have separate finances?

5. How have you seen a change in the definition of marriage over the last ten to twenty years? Will it continue?

6. Do you think becoming "one flesh" is a worthy goal?

7. Is marriage being held in honor by all?

8. Are families more complex than they were ten to twenty years ago in your opinion?

Chapter 9 – THEIR

1. Who are the "THEIRS" in your life?

2. Do you believe the American public is being played like a fiddle?

3. How well are you "standing your ground" for God's truth?

4. How is the dividing line between good and evil emerging?

5. Do you know God's Word, the Bible, well enough to defend it?

6. How can you learn the Bible to be able to do so?

7. Is your name written in the Lamb's book of life?

8. Where will you spend eternity? Will you be taking anyone with you?

Chapter 10 – KING

1. Who or what is the king that sits on the throne of your heart?

2. What do you think of the description of Jesus Christ in Revelation?

3. Which kind of tears will you be shedding before Christ?

4. Have you ever thought about the fact that heaven and hell are both for eternity?

5. Will you be standing on the right or the left side of Jesus Christ the true King?

6. How do you praise Jesus Christ?

7. How do you mock Jesus Christ?

8. Are you prepared for the war that is coming?

Chapter 11 – ?

1. How are you impacting your family and others around you for Christ?

2. How does life seem to be going by fast?

3. Are you thinking from an eternal or a temporal perspective?

4. Do you think man or God is in control of everything?

5. How are you relying on your own power and strength?

6. How will you have to answer for the raising of your kids?

7. How is your life "relevant" for Jesus Christ?

8. Will the work of your life be burnt up? Or will it be lasting for eternity?

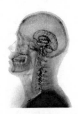

BIBLIOGRAPHY

Life Application Study Bible. Carol Stream: Tyndale House Publishers. Grand Rapids: Zondervan, 2005.

Geisler, Norman. *I Don't Have Enough Faith to be an Atheist.* Wheaton: Crossway, 2004.

Ham, Ken. Already Gone: *Why your kids will quit Church and what you can do to stop it.* Forest: Master Books, 2009.

MacArthur, John. *Ashamed of the Gospel: When the Church Becomes Like the World.* Wheaton: Crossway, 2010.

MacArthur, John. *Because the Time is Near: John MacArthur Explains the Book of Revelation.* Chicago: Moody, 2007.

MacArthur, John. *The Gospel According to Jesus: What Is Authentic Faith?* Grand Rapids: Zondervan, 1994.

MacArthur, John. Slave: *The Hidden Truth About Your Identity in Christ.* Nashville: Thomas Nelson, 2010.

MacArthur, John. *Nothing But the Truth: Upholding the Gospel in a Doubting Age.* Wheaton: Crossway, 2008.

MacArthur, John. *Saved without a Doubt: Being Sure About your Salvation*. Colorado Springs: David C Cook, 2011.

MacArthur, John. *The Truth War: Fighting for Certainty in an Age of Deception*. Nashville: Thomas Nelson, 2010.

Murray, Andrew. *The Essential Works of Andrew Murray*. Uhrichsville: Barbour Publishing, 2008.

Stanley, Andy. *The Principle of the Path: How to Get from Where You Are to Where You Want to Be*. Nashville: Thomas Nelson, 2008.

Tozer, A.W. *The Crucified Life: How To Live Out a Deeper Christian Experience*. Ventura: Regal, 2011.

Tozer, A.W. *The Dangers of a Shallow Faith: Awakening from Spiritual Lethargy*. Ventura: Regal, 2012

Tozer, A.W. *Experiencing the Presence of God: Teachings From the Book of Hebrews*. Ventura: Regal, 2010

Tozer, A.W. *God's Power for Your Life: How the Holy Spirit Transforms You Through God's Word*. Ventura: Regal, 2013.

Tozer, A.W. *The Knowledge of the Holy*. New York: Harper Collins, 1961

Tozer, A.W. *The Warfare of the Spirit: Religious Ritual Versus the Presence of the Indwelling Christ*. Camp Hill: Wing Spread Publishers, 2006.

Zacharias, Ravi. *The Grand Weaver: How God Shapes Us Through the Events of Our Lives*. Grand Rapids: Zondervan, 2007.

MARK'S SCRIPTURE REFERENCES

1. Proverbs 1:7 – Are we fools? Or wise?
2. Proverbs 3:5-6 – Who do you trust – you or God?
3. Jeremiah 29:11-13 – God has a plan for your life!
4. Romans 7:4, Ephesians 2:10 – Why are we here?
5. 1 John 1:8-9 – We must confess our sins!
6. Joshua 1:8 – Meditate on God's Word daily!
7. 2 Timothy 3:16-17 – The Scriptures teach us.
8. Romans 3:20-31 – The "Heart" of the Gospel!
9. Revelation 3:20 – We must open the door!
10. Philippians 3:7-14 – Press-on to the upward call!
11. Galatians 2:20 – We have been crucified with Christ!
12. John 14:6, Acts 4:12, 1 John 5:11-12, 1Timothy 2:5 – Jesus is the ONLY way of salvation we have!
13. Romans 12:1-2 – Renewing of our mind transforms us.
14. Galatians 5:22-23 – The fruit of the Spirit, ask for it!
15. Matthew 6:25-34 – Do not worry!!!!!!!!!!!!!!
16. Philippians 4:6-8 – Rejoice and don't be anxious!
17. Philippians 4:11-13 – Be content in everything!
18. Romans 5:1-5 – At the end of all suffering is hope!
19. Romans 8:28 – In all things, God works for the good!
20. Romans 8:37-39 – Nothing can separate us from Christ!
21. Psalms 1, 22, 23, 27, 51, 53, 69, 73, 91, 103, 111, 119, 138, 139
22. Hebrews 11 – The "Faith" chapter
23. Matthew 5-7 – The Sermon on the Mount
24. Ephesians – We believers are the body of Christ!
25. Ephesians 1:4 – God chose us!
26. Ephesians 2:8-9 – We are saved by grace!
27. Psalm 119:67-72, 105 – God's Word is a lamp to our feet!
28. Proverbs – The book of Wisdom!
29. 1 Corinthians 1:18 – The foolish perish!
30. Philippians 2:3-11 – Be an humble servant!
31. 1 Peter 2:9-10 – We as Christians are a royal priesthood!
32. 1 Peter 2:24 – Jesus Christ bore our sins!
33. 1 Peter 5:6-10 – God restores us!
34. Matthew 22:37-40 – The two great commandments!
35. Matthew 7:21-23 – One of the scariest verses in the Bible – Not all who think and say they are Christians are going to heaven!
36. Matthew 25:21 & 34 – The words we all long to hear!
37. Colossians 1:10-12 – My prayer for you!
38. Colossians 2:8 – Do not be deceived!!!!!!!!!!!!!
39. 1 Thessalonians 4:13-5:11 – Will you be left behind?
40. Matthew 25:31-46 – Eternal punishment vs. Eternal life in heaven – we will all be at one or the other!
41. 1 Thessalonians 5:16-18 – Thou shalt not BELLYACHE!!!!!!
42. 2 Thessalonians 1:8-10 – Jesus – the ONLY way to avoid destruction!
43. John 3:35-36 – Eternal life with Jesus or God's wrath – which will you receive?
44. 2 Thessalonians 2:9-12 – Some will be deceived and perish!
45. Romans 1:20 – We are without excuse!
46. John 14:15, 21, 23 – If we love Jesus, we obey Him!
47. Isaiah 55:8-9 – God's thoughts and ways are higher than ours!
48. Hebrews 7:24-25 – Jesus intercedes for His saints!
49. John 17 – The Holy of Holies!
50. Matthew 10:32-33 – Don't be ashamed of Jesus!
51. Ephesians 6:10-18 – Put on the full armor of GOD!